TIME TO
MOVE ON

THE 7 CAREER MYTHS
Keeping You From Finding
Your Dream Job...

And What to
Do About It

MUSTAFA AMMAR

ISBN: 979-8-218-16537-6

Book Cover & Layout: Summer R. Morris
www.SumoDesignStudio.com

PRAISE FOR *TIME TO MOVE ON*

"Pursuing your passion and finding your dream career is the ultimate goal that you should be seeking. Mustafa exposes all the hidden myths that you should bust before finding your dream career. *Time to Move On!* is the right answer to your career's hopes."

—Dr. Ivan Misner, Founder of BNI
New York Times Bestselling Author

"This book will inspire and motivate you like no other. Chock-full of great stories, Mustafa dispels the common "career myths." It's the first book that really gives you permission to pursue the career of your dreams—now! Learn how to quiet your inner voice and silence the thunderous crowds of outer critics, including your closest friends and family members. Learn how to step out of your comfort zone and thrive in your new zone of learning and growth. A master storyteller, Mustafa walks you through his own amazingly successful yet wildly diverse careers, from pharmacist to diplomat, banker, entrepreneur and beyond. This book is a *must read* for anyone entering the job market, stuck in a job they hate, or starting the next chapter of their life after retirement."

—June Ryan, Rear Admiral, U.S. Coast Guard, MA Ed.

"Early on Mustafa emphasizes one of my favorite quotes, "The only constant is change." Many in the career space are predicting that over half the jobs and career choices and fields in the next ten to twenty years do not yet exist today. So why should you be locked out of these opportunities? Mustafa encourages you to explore your passions and seize opportunities. In *Time to Move On* Mustafa masterfully argues that as humans, we are wired for change. He inspires us to embrace the change that pursuing these new roles provide and to *never give up*. Mustafa is living proof of following the path of your passions—and he shows you the way. As he suggests, don't get too comfortable and complacent. I thoroughly enjoyed his insights. I have no doubt you will too!"

—Scott Dell, CPA, CPC, DBA, PhD.
Assistant Professor of Accounting, Francis Marion University
Chief Inspiration Officer, Future Forward Academy

"Armed with captivating storytelling and research-backed statistics, Mustafa attacks the 7 career myths that hold professionals back from pursuing their most fulfilling work. Each chapter leads you from your comfort zone, toward a learning and growth mindset. The book is filled with inspiring and personable stories and will test your long-held assumptions about career switching. After finishing this book, you will have a new understanding of why and how to make a meaningful and purposeful career transition."

—Lisa Spinelli, ACC, Career Coach

"In coaching people with career issues and going through career changes for over 20 years, I have heard every one of the seven career myths that Mustafa addresses in his book. His keen insights ring true in the real world of career growth and shapeshifting. This is an extraordinarily insightful book by an extraordinarily interesting man. Mustafa's journey and what he has learned through experience is a must read for anyone feeling trapped in their career—but especially for anyone ready to break free and experience life in a whole new way."

—Steven B Welling,
Coach and Consultant with Strategic Mentor

"Mustafa has written a wonderful book that inspires us with his own personal stories and practical advice. He dismantles the myths that create the barriers standing in the way of change. Through his own multiple career changes, Mustafa demonstrates that he understands the psychology and fear we all face, and offers the perfect amount of encouragement to 'Move On.'"

—Tamara Lashchyk, Career Expert
Host of *Next Level Life Series* Summit

"I could not put this book down. Mustafa has created a guide not just for career development, but for life. His warmth and wisdom come through on every page. Always keep this book handy. Refer to it often, and you will achieve life-changing results. Guaranteed."

—Eric Jackier, Professional Development Coach and Mentor
Author of *The Crystal-Clear Leader*

"Mustafa explains—and then dispels—seven myths that most of us have wrongly believed to be rules for success. He has walked the walk pursuing his own dreams, from pharmacist to international diplomat, investment banker, app developer, business success coach, entrepreneur, and now author. Friends and family tried to talk him out of these career moves, but he wisely listened to his gut and is now living his best life—he wants to help you do the same. Well-researched with fascinating historical references, and full of many inspiring real-life stories, *Time to Move On!* will educate and inspire you to pursue your own dreams no matter your current situation."

—Alaria Taylor, Certified Canfield Trainer in the Success Principles

"Mustafa shows us how, by shifting our mindsets and embracing career shapeshifting, a good life can become even greater. Career shapeshifters are willing to push aside fears and take calculated risks. They are willing to trust and listen to their heart, and focus on possibilities rather than limitations. The payoff is far greater than remaining in the comfort zone of certainty and security. Mustafa demonstrates this first-hand, sharing his own stories as a career shapeshifter. *Time to Move On!* is a powerful read, and will significantly expand your perspective in becoming aware of the greater possibilities that await you. Highly recommended!"

—Susan Hayes, CEO & Founder of Active Abundance

"What a great inspiration this book is! I have been confronted with many of these career myths over the course of my life—for decades, some of them kept me from finding my calling and pursuing my dreams. I love how Mustafa systematically dismantles the myths that hold back so many of us from living our dreams. His book invites us to rethink old patterns and inspires us to (re)start dreaming big and living our dreams and passions, no matter our age. It is an essential read for young people, inspiring them to live a life of their dreams."

—Julica Ortlinghaus, Lawyer, Transformational Trainer
Founder of *Passport to Shine: A Youth Empowerment Program*

"Mustafa takes you on a fascinating journey to busting all the hidden career myths that most people still believe in. It is a must-read for anybody who is stuck in their career and aspires to reach their full potential. I wish I had had a copy of *Time to Move On* when I was younger, but as a fifty-something year-old entrepreneur, the lessons are still applicable!"

—Catherine Engmann, Entrepreneur and
Certified Canfield Trainer in the Success Principles

"*Time to Move On!* is an inspiring, thought-provoking, easy-to-read book that invites you to expand your vision into infinite possibilities. If you feel stuck in a job that no longer fulfils you, if you want a career change but are afraid of making less money or losing your status quo, if you lack support to pursue a new dream—this book is for you. Mustafa debunks myths and fears around career change at any age and circumstances. He presents a new and refreshing perspective that is aligned with today's world. And he challenges you to not settle for anything less than your given potential. No matter how old you are or where you come from, you'll feel empowered to explore new opportunities, leverage your expertise to develop new skills, and design your life in a manner that's more passionate, interesting, and fulfilling to *you*."

—Laura Figueroa, Inspirational Speaker, Facilitator
Author of *From Oppression to Liberation*

"What an inspiring read! This book is packed with powerful messages. Mustafa has an admirable ability to take challenging situations and turn them into productive opportunities. If you are looking to upgrade your market value and decide on your own next big career move, I highly recommend *Time to Move On.*"

—Addy M. Kujawa, CAE, DES, CEO, The Radical Change Group
and The American Alliance of Orthopaedic Executives

"Mustafa's book is a great read if you're considering embarking on making changes in your work. It dispels the most important myths that keep professionals stuck and includes digestible examples that help you put his words into actions."

—Lucia Knight, MD Midlife Unstuck
and Career Satisfaction Designer

"As a person with almost 30 years of iterations of my career path, Mustafa's insights ring essential and true. The myths we tell ourselves to keep us "safe" and "stable" are mindset prisons that we create to hold ourselves back from living passionate, creative, whole lives. As I started reading each of his seven myths, I found myself murmuring "Yes", and "That one too." I spent at least ten years hung up on Myth 4, seemingly unable to make a change in my life. What I love most about *Time to Move On!* is not just that it calls out the self-talk many of us have experienced, but that Mustafa advocates passionately and clearly for us to overcome those feelings through action—and provides personal examples and guidance on doing it."

—Jenn Colby, Agricultural Educator
Co-founder, Whole Human Healing & Transformation

One dollar from the sale of each copy
of *Time to Move On* will be dedicated to coaching
orphaned children between the ages of 13 and
18, with the goal of helping them realize their
own dream careers. Mustafa Ammar and his
organization, The Passion MBA, are dedicated to
training and coaching one million children by 2030.

For more information on this effort,

please contact

dreamcareer@thepassionmba.com.

"You don't choose your family. They are God's gift to you, as you are to them."

— DESMOND TUTU

To my family:
I won't be the same person without you.
God bless you!

To Taha,
my childhood friend,
who always believed in me:
RIP

TABLE OF CONTENTS

FOREWORD
by Jack Canfield

America's # 1 Success Coach and
New York Times Bestselling Coauthor of
The Success Principles™ and the *Chicken Soup for the Soul®* Series

*F*irst of all, congratulations for choosing to read this book—Time *to Move On.* You are in good hands because Mustafa Ammar has made several major career transitions over the course of his life, and his insights on when, how, and why he needed to move on are invaluable.

I have known Mustafa for quite some time now, and I have to say he is one of the most interesting people I have ever met. He is a real polymath who has lived several career lives, which have educated and informed his life and his professional journey. He has been a pharmacist and then an international diplomat who worked and lived in China for ten years. Mustafa has also been an investment banker focusing on business development in several regions around the world. And more recently, as an entrepreneur and a career coach, he has been very successful in helping people transform their lives by helping them discover their life purposes, pursue their passions, and find their dream careers.

Over the last few years, Mustafa has worked with me in several of my training programs including my Success Principles Train the Trainer certification program, our Executive Retreats, and our Breakthrough to Success trainings. As a result he has successfully merged The Success Principles with his Passion Blueprint to help people find their dream careers.

On a personal level, we have had numerous conversations on international political issues, Chinese culture, and Egyptian history, to our spiritual practices, and even our favorite movies.

Mustafa is what I call a powerful myth buster. In the era of "The Great Resignation," when millions of people in America and around the world are willingly resigning from their jobs, it has become crucial to highlight Mustafa's work in helping professionals rediscover themselves, find their lost passions, and bust the most common, yet most hidden career myths. In *Time to Move On*, Mustafa shatters much of the conventional wisdom and all the traditional career assumptions. For example, you don't have to specialize in one single tiny specialization in order to succeed in life. Or you don't have to focus only on your strengths to excel in your career. In such a time of massive disruption in our history, we need more Myth Busters like Mustafa who can help people to find their true calling.

So, if you are one of these millions that are fueling the massive movement of The Great Resignation, or if you are contemplating joining it soon, I strongly encourage you to keep reading *Time to Move On* and learn how to bust these career myths before making any career move.

ACKNOWLEDGMENTS

Writing a book is a long journey full of inspiration, discovery, and self-exploration. Along the way, I got to know dozens of people who helped me. Chronologically, I have to start with my Brazilian friends Bruno Shigemura, Leduar Staniscia, and Edson Ferreira, all of whom inspired me to write this book. We met for the first time over a dim sum dinner while attending a venture capital workshop in Hong Kong in March of 2019. When I told them my story, their response was: "You have to write a book and tell your story to the world." Since then, they sent me dozens of messages encouraging me to write it. The last one was from Bruno: "Still waiting for you to publish that book, mate."

Obrigado meus amigos—without you and your continuous encouragement, I wouldn't be here.

After reading Tim Ferriss' brilliant book *The 4-hour Work a Week* three times, my life and way of thinking changed. Even more than that, Tim introduced me to both Jack Canfield and Steve Harrison when I watched their iconic interview with Tim. Thank you, Tim.

I'm eternally grateful to Jack Canfield, without a doubt, the best success coach in America as well as *The New York Times* Bestselling author of *Chicken Soup for The Soul*. Jack was with me from the first time I envisioned writing this book and dreaming about being a bestselling author. I discovered Jack through his interview with Tim, and he has been invaluable guiding me through the process of becoming an author. Since those early days, he has always been there for me. I was lucky to get the chance to participate in his private mastermind retreat, as well as his "Breakthrough to Success" and "Train the Trainer" events. Through these experiences, Jack shared dozens of invaluable insights with me on the book you are reading as well as my next one. He was kind enough to write the foreword to this book. Thank you, Jack, my spiritual father, for being a great mentor and guide during this journey.

A huge thank-you to my mentor Patty Aubrey, bestselling author and president of Jack Canfield Companies. Patty is the mastermind behind the phenomenal success of The Canfield Group. Thank you for having so much faith in me. I feel so lucky to be part of your Mastermind Men's Group, where I have had the chance to meet brilliant and high-achieving entrepreneurs and authors. Having you as a continuous presence in my entrepreneurship journey has been a huge blessing.

Dr. Ivan Misner, bestselling author and the founder and Chief Visionary Officer of the Business Networking Organization (BNI), has been an invaluable mentor. Ivan has supported me since we first met at one of Jack Canfield's events. Despite his busy schedule running the biggest networking organization in the world, he supported me and this book beyond what I would have ever expected. Thank you, Ivan, for trusting me and trusting that this book can change people's lives.

Steve Harrison, CEO of Bradley Communications, one of the foremost publicity experts in the world, provided invaluable guidance and support. He helped me market my book and build more publicity and media exposure for my coaching business. Steve's "National Publicity Summit" was a game changer for me— it opened a whole new world and it helped me secure dozens of media interviews that gave me the opportunity to talk about my book and unique coaching methodology. Thank you, Steve.

To me and many other fellow authors, Geoffrey Berwind is the best story-telling expert in the world. I got to know Geoffrey when I was just transitioning into coaching and considered writing a sign from God that I am destined for this amazing journey. No one has ever believed in me as much as Geoffrey has. I'm extremely fortunate to have him as one of my best friends and mentors. He helped me craft my story, including my signature story included in the introduction of this book. Together, we wrote dozens of stories of people who were able to transform their lives by changing their careers —all of these stories (including Geoffrey's) will be featured in my next book. I enjoyed your guided tour of the Italian District in Philadelphia, the Museum of Art, and visiting every place the legendary movie *Rocky* was filmed. Thank you, Geoffrey. I am blessed to have you in my life, my friend.

I could not have written this book without my amazing New York book coach, author and editor Debra Englander. I got to work with Debby in 2020 through Steve Harrison's program, "Get Published Now." Debby has been a huge asset in my journey. She helped me to craft every chapter of the book using her decades of experiences in writing and editing books. Thanks to Debby, I was also able to reach out to—and interview—dozens of bestselling authors and entrepreneurs who will be included in my next book.

More importantly, Debby introduced me to Cynthia Zigmund, Founder and President of Second City Publishing Services.

This book would not have seen the light of day without Cynthia. I am so lucky to work with one of the most professional and experienced people I have ever met in my life. With all the complexities that this project has been through, working with Cynthia made it smooth and flexible. I am astonished by the level of professionalism, trust, and understanding that I received from her. Moreover, this book wouldn't be as professional as it is now without her guidance and support. Cynthia helped me to carefully develop my stories in a plausible and attractive way. She also made sure that the conversations and dialogues within the book were powerful and interactive. As Debby once told me, "You are in good hands with Cynthia."

Successful people always work in teams and I was lucky to work with Cynthia's team. A big shout-out to Rachel Shuster, my book's copyeditor. Rachel was the first person to prove to me that editing a book can be a very interesting and smooth job. Rachel has a very magical way to find the perfect word in the right context. Summer Morris did a great job in designing the book's interior and cover. Cynthia, Summer, and I spent weeks revising several versions of the cover until the three of us felt great about the final cover. I appreciate their patience with me, their understanding to my needs, and their professionalism in working hard to create a top quality work, one that I will be proud of the rest of my life.

A big thank you to my executive assistant, Ijnwaa Ceniza, who did a lot of supporting research to help me bring some fresh data and insights to this book, especially in Myth 1.

Author Chris Guillebeau inspired me to be the person I am. I got to know Chris's work at a very pivotal moment in my life. His books changed my life in less than a year! After reading *The $100 Startup* during a quick birthday holiday at Discovery Bay in Hong Kong, I went out and bought all his books and finished them in nine months. I still remember my big "aha" moment, while reading *Born for This* in London: it was when I made the decision to leave my banking and diplomacy careers behind me to become a career coach. I feel that we have a connection since I almost traveled to the same African and Asian countries that he traveled to, with the same attitude for adventure. I am forever grateful to you, Chris.

I read author David Epstein's book *Range* at a very pivotal moment in my life—when I was considering transitioning from being a banker to becoming an author, coach, and entrepreneur. I was not sure if I should follow my new passion or just stick with my banking career. David's book proved to me that a generalist can triumph in a specialized world. David, I owe you so much and I am sure we "polymathy advocates" will change the world.

Although, I don't read much fiction, Paulo Coelho's *The Alchemist* is my favorite book by far. If you can read just one book, after holy books, make it *The Alchemist*. It's a must-read for anyone who has dreams. I saw myself in the Andalusian boy Santiago in his journey to the Pyramids of Egypt searching for his own personal legend. I read (or listened to) the story dozens of times, and I'm still reading it, especially when I feel down and need some encouragement. I learned that "In order to find the treasure, you will have to follow the omens. And God has prepared a path for everyone to follow. You just have to read the omens that he left for you." I am eternally grateful to you, Paulo.

Organizational psychologist Adam Grant's books were very inspiring to me. Reading his book *Originals* gave me the permission I needed to act as a non-conformist who always wants to change the world. I realized that as a nonconformist, I have a responsibility to take a different path from the masses and lead. Thanks to Adam, I am taking that different path—and leading.

Motivational speaker Chris Gardner's story was (and remains) a major source of inspiration to me. His autobiography *The Pursuit of Happyness* (also a great movie) taught me to never give up. Whenever I encounter a tough situation and am so frustrated I just want to walk away, I think of Chris Gardner and I remind myself that if a homeless, single father could succeed in his pursuits, why can't I? Thanks, Chris.

Sylvester Stallone and Rocky Balboa, the character he portrayed in the film *Rocky*, taught me an early lesson in life: Don't give up. Even if you get hardly hit, get up and fight back again. Watching Rocky's training scenes in the streets of Philadelphia, the film helped me build a resilient mindset, and taught me the importance of never giving up without a fight. I still watch those scenes regularly to recharge my "resilience" batteries. Thank you, Rocky Balboa.

And finally, a shout-out to Tom Hanks, Meg Ryan, the late Nora Ephron, and everybody else who was involved with the film *Sleepless in Seattle*. This is my favorite movie—it inspired and taught me to read the signs and learn that destiny always has a hand in the journeys we take. I have watched this movie hundreds of times (even more than *Rocky*) and still watch it when I want to affirm to myself that destiny takes a hand.

INTRODUCTION
YOUR FUTURE DEPENDS ON...
YOU!

My mind had descended into complete chaos—it was totally disorganized and confused. Physically, my lips started to tremble and my hands began to shake. My one hand clenched my pen with a death's grip, as if my entire future depended on it.

In fact, it did.

I had been preparing for, and anticipating, this day for years. And yet, here I was staring at a blank piece of paper, unable to write down what I had spent so much time preparing for—the most important exam of my life. If I wanted to fulfill my dream to become an international diplomat, I needed to pass this exam.

There was no going back—I *couldn't* fail this test.

Becoming a diplomat had been my dream since I was twelve years old, when I immersed myself in reading about history and geography, memorizing the capitals of the world, and learning all I could. I was intent on becoming a diplomat—my goal consumed my thoughts and aspirations.

But a few years later, my journey was interrupted. As is typical with most teenagers, I developed new interests and was confused about what I wanted to pursue: I loved diplomacy but didn't want to commit to studying political theory and economics. Instead, when I turned sixteen, I decided to study chemistry out of a sudden desire to become a pharmacist. Fast-forward seven years to when I was twenty-three and about to graduate with a major in pharmaceutical sciences: my passion for diplomacy resurfaced, stronger than before.

But I stuck to my plan and graduated, and then began working as a pharmacist. However, my urge for becoming a diplomat didn't ebb and I spent nights and weekends studying global affairs, economics, and international law. I improved my written and spoken English and French language skills to fluent levels. At the same time, I was saving as much as I could from my modest salary to invest in courses I began taking to help me achieve my goal of becoming a diplomat.

As I began to study and prepare for my new career, doubts and discouraging thoughts began to creep in on a daily basis: "I just graduated and now I'm looking to move to a new career already? What am I doing? Why don't I just settle down and focus on getting a better salary, or a better position in a bigger company, or even build my own pharmacy? Can't I see how ridiculous this looks to the people around me?"

I began to question everything.

I was at war with myself.

My passion for diplomacy was overtaking my new career. I was obsessed with becoming a diplomat, so I could represent my culture and travel the world. Practicing pharmacy had become a cage that I needed to escape from!

I kept plugging away at my studies until the big moment arrived: the exam which would decide my fate and my future. I knew it would be a difficult experience. I would be tested on eleven subjects over five successive days, and I had to pass them all. The toughest part was seeing people around me dropping out after the first day of testing because they knew they hadn't passed the first exam. More people dropped out on the third day because they could not pass the second round of exams. I managed to finish the five days with what I felt were reasonable answers and had high hopes of making it to the next stage, the final interview.

I had to wait six months to get my results. Finally, I received the answer: I had failed to pass. The news weighed heavily on my soul, and I was devastated. As I tried to figure out what went wrong, in my mind I kept hearing the ridicule from people who had discouraged me from pursuing a career in diplomacy: "We told you this would happen. You wasted your time. You should have listened to us!"

At that point, I realized I needed to figure out what I should do next: give up my dream or try again and apply for the next exam. I decided to take some time by myself to decide—away from external influences and distractions—and spent a month distancing myself from those around me. Instead, I focused on working and reflecting. I prayed for guidance and looked within for advice. Finally, the voice within me became clear: "This is your passion. This is your dream. Do you want to give it up and be miserable, or try your best and not have to regret pursuing your passion? There must be a reason behind all of this, and you should not stop trying to reach for your dreams." I listened to that voice carefully, and after a month of reflection, I knew I had to try again. This time I wouldn't leave any room for failure.

Ever since I was a kid, I have always had a "don't give up attitude"—it's part of who I am. I still remember the first time I watched the now-famous scene in the film *Rocky* when Sylvester Stallone's character was training and running in the streets of Philadelphia, surrounded by kids who were trying to keep up. I was five years old at the time and imagined myself being one of those kids. I didn't have much understanding of things at that time, but I felt something inside me that was positive, powerful, and significant. The scene, accompanied by the equally famous song "Gonna Fly Now," fueled my desire, grit, and perseverance. I enjoyed the parts of the film when Rocky got knocked down but managed to get up and fight until he won. *Rocky* taught me to never give up.

In a way, *Rocky* inspired me to listen to my heart and try again. I started working even harder on my preparation. I decided to work part-time so I could devote more time to studying. Barely a month before the exam, I resigned from my job to give it my all.

The big day arrived, and the first two exams went well. But, by the third night I was so exhausted and sleep-deprived that I decided to take a sleeping pill, so I could get some sleep for the first time in a week. The next day, when I started the exam, I was shocked to find that none of the essay questions I had prepared for were part of the exam. Fortunately, after taking hundreds of exams over the years, I knew that I needed to stay calm, resilient, and focused. Unfortunately, thirty minutes in, things got worse. Much worse. The effect of too many sleepless nights and the sleeping pill I had taken caused my whole body to start shivering—my lips began to tremble and my hands froze. I didn't know what was happening to me and was obsessed with not wanting to fail the exam.

Soon, other people started noticing that I was in bad shape. They even arranged a visit from a physician, but he couldn't help me. I was given some water, but I couldn't hold the glass because my hands were shaking so hard, so they put some drops in my mouth. Others brought me some candy for energy. Nothing seemed to help.

I was at the end of my rope and prayed: "This is my last chance, God. I did my best to prepare for this day. Please, God, if this is not my destiny for a reason and wisdom that You know, I accept it. But I won't let go of this pen. I will hold onto it with whatever power I still have in my body!"

Squeezing the pen with my hand was all I could do. That pen represented everything up to that moment: my dreams, my passions, and my hopes for the future. I clenched that pen and forced myself to slowly, painfully, compose my essays. To this day, I don't know how I did it, but I managed to write full essays with hardly any physical strength and just a fraction of my brain functioning.

After the exam, some of my colleagues helped me downstairs, where I met my father. We drove home in silence because I couldn't talk. Once home, I slept better than I had for weeks.

That experience taught me one of my biggest life lessons:

If you really want something, do your best and leave the rest to God. You can't do everything on our own, and He won't help you until you fight for it first.

If you really want something,

do your best and leave the

rest to God. You can't do everything

on our own, and

He won't help you until

you fight for it first.

Introdcution: Your Future Depends On... You!

More than nine months after that experience—having taken eleven written exams, as well as a series of interviews and IQ tests—I received the news that I had been chosen as one of thirty new diplomats out of almost two thousand candidates. I'm convinced that if I had given up my pen that day, I wouldn't be sharing my experiences with you today. Instead, I would be living another life that was not authentically mine. But by holding on tightly and giving it all that I had, I passed the test. And I don't just mean the diplomacy test: I mean the *life* test that I went through that day. Life was waiting to see if I would hold on tightly to my pen—my hopes and dreams—and be rewarded, or give up and fail.

Here's the lesson I want you to take away from what I've shared with you so far:

Listen to your heart and don't settle: hold on to your dreams and don't give up something you are passionate about. Don't live your life according to what others expect from you. Hold on to whatever you define as your "pen" as tightly as you can. And don't give it up. Ever.

This story and others you'll read in this book are about falling, failure, suffering, self-doubt, pain, and low self-esteem. You'll read about being underestimated and underrated. But these are also stories of faith, hope, endurance, persistence, consistency, praying, humility, success, and conquering dreams and overcoming challenges. And what in life is more fulfilling than conquering and realizing your dreams?

The stories in this book are ones you might experience yourself one day. I will be sharing what I have been through across my own life journey as a shy, introverted kid who dared to dream, and

Listen to your heart and don't settle:

hold on to your dreams and don't

give up something you are passionate

about. Don't live your life according

to what others expect from you. Hold

on to whatever you define as your

"pen" as tightly as you can.

And don't give it up. Ever.

went on to become a pharmacist, diplomat, investment banker, entrepreneur, career coach, author, app developer, and who knows what else! My hope is that you find my stories enlightening, inspiring, and life-changing. Have you ever been in a situation where most of the people around you question or even ridicule your dreams and your ability to achieve them? These situations can prove to be a very dark moment in time. I experienced my own share of dark moments. I suffered a lot while trying to listen to my heart, pursue my own passions, and live my own dreams instead of what others were expecting of me. In the coming pages, I will be sharing the wisdom I learned from my often roller coaster of a journey. My hope is that this little book will help you build the wisdom, inspiration, and enlightenment you need to be the hero of your own story.

THE 7 CAREER MYTHS

"Twenty years from now you will be more disappointed by the things you didn't do than by the ones you did do. So throw off the bowlines. Sail away from the safe harbor. Catch the trade winds in your sails.

Explore. Dream. Discover."

— MARK TWAIN

If you want to live a happy and fulfilled life, and enjoy a career that can have a positive impact on yourself and the people around you, I have good news for you! I have been there, not just once, but four times. I did it the hard way and without any guidance or a blueprint to follow. I only had my dream, hopes for my future, and faith in God. I spent hundreds of nights questioning my dreams and doubting my ability to achieve them, but my hope and faith became a beacon of light in a sea of darkness. If I knew then what I know now, things would have been so much easier. I'm not complaining: the journey was worth it in order to fulfill my dreams!

Consider your life or career as a project. Many of us build our careers or lives on weak foundations, resulting in deterioration or even collapse at some point. Some of us build our careers and lives on the wrong foundations, and the outcomes are even worse. We spend most of our lives trying to constantly make repairs to those faulty foundations. The wise among us build our careers and lives using the right footings—as a result, we can build skyscrapers or even pyramids that last longer than we do. In other words, the impacts of the choices we make can outlive us and benefit others who come after us.

An example of a weak foundation is building your career on something you are not passionate about, resulting in career burnout and no motivation to make a change—you become apathetic. An example of a wrong foundation is a career based on a short-lived trend or one factor (such as money) instead of looking at the complete picture. A weak or wrong foundation may not crumble completely, but it won't support you as effectively as it should. The first step toward building the best foundation is to bust some career myths.

Most of us grew up being taught that the myths we'll be exploring are actually rules for success, when in reality, they are anything but. Building your life and career based on myths means you are wasting the one and only life you have, by heeding bad advice. It took me years to discover these "rules" were actually myths, and that I had wasted my time believing in them. But at the same time, I am thankful and proud that I was able to decipher those myths and expose them as fake and inauthentic. I was fortunate that my awakening happened early in my life, so I could go on to live a fulfilled life, pursuing my passions and realizing my life's purpose. As a myth buster, I'm going to share what I learned, so you don't need to waste your time or your entire life chasing those myths. And I promise I will continue dedicating my life to busting more myths that prevent people like you from reaching their full potential and living their dreams.

In this book, we'll bust seven career and life myths, so you can build (or rebuild) your life on a strong foundation and thrive. These are the myths I discovered over the course of four career transitions:

1. You need to be a "supreme specialist"

2. Change is too risky

3. It's too late to find your dream career

4. You have bills to pay

5. Focus on your strengths, not your weaknesses

6. Leaving your career is a "sunk cost"

7. You are already in your dream job

In the first myth (You need to be a "supreme specialist"), I will show you why you don't have to be a specialist in one narrow category to be successful in your career and life. We'll explore why life from the other side—as a generalist, a polymath (a person of encyclopedic learning, as we'll delve into shortly), or a career shapeshifter™—is much more interesting. Specialization is fine for bees and ants, but humans were created differently. We need to explore different pursuits and dreams. I will also show you that the magic happens, but *only* when you have enough dots to connect across seemingly unrelated careers or domains.

In the second myth (*Change is too risky*), I will show you that change is not your enemy. In fact, change is good—and essential. The only constant in life is change. Everything changes, including you. I'll show you why change should be your best friend, as it is for me. We'll explore how to anticipate it, embrace it, and seize it before it seizes you. By opening your mindset toward changes that happen to you, you give yourself an opportunity to explore what you never imagined exploring.

In the third myth (*It's too late to find your dream career*), we'll explore why there is no better time to pursue your dreams than *now*. No matter how old you are, you can reach for your dreams—it's never too late. We'll learn why people in their sixties and seventies are able to change their lives, while younger people get stuck.

In the fourth myth (*You have bills to pay*), we will bust one of the most overused excuses for giving up: "I have to pay my bills." This sentence drives me crazy. I have heard it hundreds of times from people who use it to disqualify themselves from achieving their dreams and living the life they deserve. I'll show you how to take a step-by-step approach to find your dream career, while still being able to pay your bills.

In the fifth myth (*Focus on your strengths, not your weaknesses*), we'll bust the old belief that it's better and easier to work on your strengths than to work on your weaknesses. In fact, sometimes it is easier for you to work on your weaknesses than your strengths. We'll explore how successful people and high achievers look carefully at their weaknesses *before* they even look at the strengths. I'll show you how focusing on your weaknesses is a victory for your growth mindset versus a fixed and complacent mindset that focuses only on strengthening your strengths.

In the sixth myth (*Leaving your career is a sunk cost*), I will show you why leaving your career is not a "sunk cost" (that is, a waste of what you've already invested in yourself). Transitioning to a new career doesn't mean you've wasted your skills or your experiences; I will show you how to transfer and transmute all your experiences and skills so you can pursue your dream career and follow your passions.

And finally in the seventh myth (*You are already in your dream job*), we will bust the "this is the best job in the world" myth. I will show you how to enjoy every career or job that you have, while understanding that you may have more than one dream or passion in life. I'll even demonstrate how to become a *career shapeshifter*™ who is able to transition and live several dream careers in a single life.

Are you ready to bust some myths? Let's get started!

MYTH #1

You Need to be a "Supreme Specialist"

People who are the world's topmost experts in only one tiny field are not wise in general, while people who engage themselves seriously with a number of diverse fields are often capable of deeper overviews of important and complex situations."

— DOUGLAS HOFSTADTER

The myth goes like this: You have to stick to one major in college and rush to a specialization, stick to that specialization, and get promoted until you become an expert and authority in that specialization. This is the definition of success.

"Jack of all trades, master of none." We've all heard the expression. It's what we learned in school and what our families and elders have instilled in us. It's also misleading.

Let's take a step back and ask a question: Just what is a specialist?

A specialist is someone who has a lot of experience or knowledge in a particular subject or domain. He or she is an expert in a narrow specialization and probably spent their life developing that expertise. Sounds like a definition of success, right? If being a specialist or expert is the definition of success, then someone who regularly changes his or her career would be considered unsuccessful, correct? The problem with thinking this way is that we are assuming that specialization has always existed—but that's not the case.

The word "specialist" first appeared in the English language in 1836. The word never existed before then—neither did the concept of being a specialist or an expert in a single occupation. The term was created for a reason. As the world was progressing economically, Adam Smith and other economists believed that specialization and the division of labor were essential to advancing the world economy. They believed that total output and production wouldn't increase unless workers and laborers specialized in one segment of their vocation. They believed specialization was the only way to increase world productivity exponentially.

I am not advocating against specialization. The theory makes sense and has no doubt had a massive impact on the global economy over the last two centuries. It's even likely that specialization existed before the term was coined, but in a less restricted form and without towering barriers among different domains and professions. But let's consider this question: How were we able to excel before specialization, as we know it today, existed?

The answer can be found in "polymaths." In other words, people were able to specialize, while at the same time they were free to cross the boundaries or borders between vocations. As a result, we had an abundance of "polymaths," people who were freely navigating between careers and domains, pursuing their passions and learning—without any restrictions or condemnation from the society.

On the other side, a "polymath" comes from the Greek *polys* meaning "much" and from the root of *manthanein,* a verb that refers to the process of learning. Its first recorded use in English language was in the 1620s.

Polymath is a noun that refers to a person who is well-informed and learned about a wide variety of topics, as opposed to possessing expertise in one specific field. A "Renaissance man" (or woman) is an example of a polymath, but its history goes back thousands of years.

Every civilization in history has been characterized by large numbers of polymaths; they were the ones responsible for integrating ideas and connecting concepts. Imhotep was the first known polymath in history (around 2667-2660 BC). He was an Egyptian chancellor, physician, author, and architect who built the Djoser pyramid (the first pyramid built in old Egypt), as well as several other professions.

The Greek civilization would not have been what it was without the contributions of Aristotle and his fellow polymaths. The Islamic civilization would not have been responsible for hundreds of scientific discoveries without the leading roles that Abu Ali al Hasan ibn al-Haytham and his fellow scientists played in integrating science, knowledge, and art. Notable polymaths include Hypatia, Zhang Heng, Mariam al-Astrulabi, Al-Khwarizmi, Ziryab, Shen Kuo, Leonardo da Vinci, Galileo, Mary Somerville, Benjamin

Every civilization in history has been

characterized by large numbers

of polymaths; they were the ones

responsible for integrating ideas and

connecting concepts.

Franklin, Thomas Jefferson, Marie Curie, and Maya Angelou. They all possessed an intelligence that ranged across a diversity of subjects, including science, literature, philosophy, mathematics, music, art, and more.

THE NEW POLYMATHS: CAREER SHAPESHIFTERS™

With specialization ruling the world for the past two hundred years, polymathy looks to be already extinct. But career changers—people I call "career shapeshifters™"—are the new polymaths.

Shapeshifting is a phenomenon popular with mythologists and fantasy writers. In layman's terms, it is a process of changing one's physical form to another being. The most common form of shapeshifting is known as therianthropy, where a human being is transformed into an animal. This concept has appeared in the oldest literature and survives today in fantasy novels and movies. The forms and beliefs related to shapeshifting may have changed over time, but there is a single common denominator: shapeshifting is attributed to the survival of the creature. Whether they were vampires or superheroes, the phenomenon was necessary to their survival, as well as the survival of those around them.

Obviously, we are not concerned with shapeshifters in fantasy and mythology, but instead the ones who exist in the real world—*career shapeshifters™*. These are the people who shift their career identity according to their individual circumstances and based on what their passions are. While many people assume that having expertise in a particular area helps them in the long run, career shapeshifters™ take a different approach. They see the world as a place filled with myriad opportunities. They don't make choices to just survive, but also to thrive by creating the best possible circumstances for themselves. *Career shapeshifters*™ *are ready when change hits by being able to adapt and reinvent themselves, again and again. Borrowing from fantasy fiction, they are the immortals.*

The world is always full of big changes, and those changes are opportunities for career shapeshifters™. A quick look at what happened as a result of the COVID-19 pandemic illustrates this. According to a report from S&P Global, the hardest hit industries were the airlines, oil and gas, and hospitality services. Before COVID-19, these industries were considered robust and profitable.[1] After many companies in these industries were forced to scale back, thousands of employees lost the jobs they had spent years building. Most of those jobs involved a specialized level of expertise.

In the United States alone, close to 9.6 million workers aged 16-64 lost their jobs in the first three quarters of 2020; the unemployment rate more than doubled from 3.8 percent in 2019 to 8.6 percent in 2020. But these figures showed an incomplete picture of what many people are still going through. The majority of people who lost their jobs had only one area of career expertise. Until they are able to secure a relevant position using those same skills, they will remain unemployed (or underemployed).[2] A

---

[1] Danny Haydon and Neeraj Kumar, "Industries Most and Least Impacted by COVID-19 from a Probability of Default Perspective—September 2020 Update," S&P Global, Sept. 21, 202, https://www.spglobal.com/marketintelligence/en/news-insights/blog/industries-most-and-least-impacted-by-covid19-from-a-probability-of-default-perspective-september-2020-update.

[2] Meera Navlakha, "People aren't ready to quit quitting," Mashable.com, Apr. 22, 2022, https://mashable.com/article/2022-great-resignation-continues.

Career shapeshifters™ are ready

when change hits by being able to

adapt and reinvent themselves, again

and again. Borrowing from fantasy

fiction, they are the immortals.

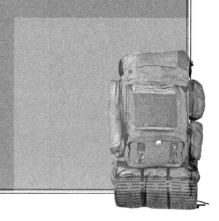

September 2020 report by Pew Research Center revealed that one in four adults were unable to pay all their bills; a third had already used up their savings; and one in six were looking to friends and family for assistance.[3] These statistics help explain the constraints and challenges that people are facing while looking for the same exact job elsewhere. Under these circumstances, career shapeshifting[TM] is more relevant than ever.

In 2022, approximately 50.5 million people quit their jobs, besting the prior record (2021).[4] The change in people's attitudes towards working represents a permanent and major shift in how we think about work. The pandemic provided an opportunity for many of us to take a hard look about what really mattered to us and our loved ones. There is no question that paying bills is important, but research has shown that the majority of the "great resignations" happened for reasons other than wanting more money:

1. A lack of passion and the need to change course

2. The need for work-life balance including spending more time with family

3. Too much toxic culture at work, including toxic bosses

4. A lack of recognition of employees by employers

5. Poor responses by organizations regarding COVID-19

---

[3] Kim Parker, Rachel Minkin, and Jesse Bennett, "Economic Fallout from COVID-19 Continues to Hit Lower-Income Americans the Hardest," Pew Research Center, Sept. 24, 2020. https://www.pewresearch.org/social-trends/2020/09/24/economic-fallout-from-covid-19-continues-to-hit-lower-income-americans-the-hardest/
[4] https://www.cnbc.com/2023/02/01/why-2022-was-the-real-year-of-the-great-resignation.html#:~:text=About%2050.5%20million%20people%20quit,to%20leave%20the%20workforce%20altogether.
[5] Ibid.

Myth #1 "You Need to Be a Supreme Specialist"

Moreover, studies shows that "the Great Resignation" doesn't show any sign of slowing down anytime soon; the hashtag #leavingmyjob has been one of the most popular hashtags on TikTok.[5] The impact of this massive move is already changing the world and is irreversible—and will be felt even if you read this book twenty or thirty years from now. The reasons behind it go beyond burnout or toxic work culture to the need for reassessing career options and redefining career success. A study in the U.S. showed that 46 percent of the participants rated passion as their top priority in their new job decision-making.[6]

The Great Resignation is not just an American phenomenon. Resignations have jumped in the United Kingdom, Australia, France and Italy,[7] while the attrition rate in the Indian IT sector is at an all-time high since the pandemic.[8]

There are many ways to address the challenges that are reshaping the job market, but in this book we're focused on how to take control by embracing career shapeshifting™. One solution would involve organizations building and supporting more inclusive

---

[6] Ariana Huffington, "People Aren't Just Quitting Their Jobs. They're Redefining Success," Inc.com, June 30, 2021, https://www.inc.com/arianna-huffington/people-arent-just-quitting-their-jobs-theyre-redefining-success.html; Jared Wadley, "Career priorities emphasize passion over financial security during pandemic," *University of Michigan News*, Feb. 1, 2022, https://news.umich.edu/career-priorities-emphasize-passion-over-financial-security-during-pandemic/.

[7] Julia Horowitz, "The Great Resignation is taking root around the world," CNN Business, Mar. 30, 2022, https://edition.cnn.com/2022/03/30/economy/great-resignation-uk-australia-europe/index.html.

[8] Sreejani Bhattacharyya, "Indian IT sector's attrition rate on the rise, no sign of respite," *Analytics India Magazine*, Mar. 9, 2022, https://analyticsindiamag.com/indian-it-sectors-attrition-rate-on-the-rise-no-sign-of-respite/#:~:text=Attrition%20in%20the%20Indian%20IT,%25%20and%2022.70%20%25%2C%20respectively.

rotation programs to allow employees to rotate and experience other roles, allowing them to follow their passions within the same organization—with the organization reaping the rewards of having developed employees who can serve in multiple roles. Also, changing recruitment strategies to include more polymath or career shapeshifters™ to allow career changers bigger space in the market has become more crucial than ever in order to stay competitive, more innovative, and disruptive.

THE BENEFITS OF BEING A CAREER SHAPESHIFTER™

Career shapeshifters™ are comfortable with being uncomfortable. Career shapeshifters™ are fast learners compared to specialists. They almost always operate in a changing environment, and they know how to handle different kinds of tasks and projects that may occur over the course of a single day. As a result, they develop an instinct for learning skills faster in order to survive and thrive. Learning new skills is a skill unto itself that needs to be developed continuously. Think of it as a muscle that needs to be trained to work and function efficiently, and to the best of its ability. *In this regard, career shapeshifters™ or polymaths have learned to be comfortable with being uncomfortable. They are always learning.*

Who do you think would be better at learning new skills? A specialist within a narrow topic who spent their entire career in that space, or someone who spent their life operating in several environments and fields?

Career shapeshifters™ can survive big crises. Career shapeshifters™ are flexible; they know how to adapt in ways

In this regard, career

shapeshifters™ or polymaths have

learned to be comfortable with

being uncomfortable. They are

always learning.

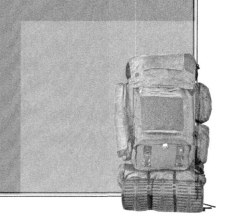

other people cannot. Think of it this way. Raccoons could be considered shapeshifters because they are able to adapt their diet to their surroundings: fruits, plants, nuts, berries, eggs, insects, crayfish, frogs, rodents, even discarded food from humans. Raccoons are adaptable, and thus have better chances of survival than other animals.

Koalas are different; they live in a specific type of forest and only eat eucalyptus leaves. This means they have next to no chance of survival when change happens to their habitat. Koalas are not naturally adaptive to the changes around them. Similarly, a specialist is less likely than a career shapeshifter™ to survive a change regardless of how well they performed in the past because they are not as adaptable and agile. When a crisis hits, a shapeshifter™ has better odds at surviving than a specialist does.

Career shapeshifters™ know how to look at the big picture while "minding the gaps." Freeman Dyson, an American mathematician and physicist, wrote about the importance of specialist frogs and polymath birds in mathematics. According to Dyson, "Birds fly high in the air and survey broad vistas of mathematics out to the far horizon."

Dyson added that frogs live in the mud below and see only the flowers that grow nearby. They delight in the details of particular objects, and they solve problems one at a time. "I happen to be a frog, but many of my best friends are birds," he said.

Dyson concluded that it is stupid to claim that birds are better than frogs because they see farther, or that frogs are better than birds because they see deeper. The world of mathematics is both broad and deep, and we need birds and frogs working together to explore it.

Myth #1 "You Need to Be a Supreme Specialist"

While specialists can see things and problems from a very narrow and deep angle, polymaths and career shapeshifters™ can see the same things from a higher and wider angle that allows them to see the bigger picture.

Peter Burke, Professor Emeritus of Cultural History at the University of Cambridge, spent years researching the power of polymaths. He stressed that in the era of specialization, polymaths are more necessary than ever, in order to bridge the gap between specialists and generalists: "It takes a polymath to 'mind the gap' and draw attention to the knowledge that may otherwise disappear into the spaces between disciplines, as they are currently defined and organized."[9]

Career shapeshifters™ are super-forecasters. In the 1950s, the philosopher Isaiah Berlin wrote an essay to differentiate two creatures: "the specialist" hedgehog and "the polymath" fox. He was inspired by Tolstoy as well as the Greek poet Archilochus, who said, "the fox knows many things, but the hedgehog knows one big thing." The fox (the polymath) has a wide understanding of many domains and a context that allows more accurate forecasting, while the hedgehog knows only one domain. As a result, while expert in one domain, the hedgehog "specialist" tends to ignore many other factors in forecasting.

Isaiah concluded that the fox doesn't just know many things. They understand that even if they "know many things," they can't possibly know everything, making them humbler and more open to listening to others. They are also willing to explore new concepts, continuously revisit their own beliefs, and consider possibilities

[9] Peter Burke, *A Social History of Knowledge II: From the Encyclopedia to Wikipedia* (Cambridge, England: Polity), 2012.

and probabilities instead of focusing on certainties. In contrast, the hedgehog won't consider other ideas. They know one big thing (their specialization) and ignore everything else.

Philip E. Tetlock, renowned psychologist and professor of leadership at Haas School of Business, University of California Berkley, launched his two-decades long study "Expert Political Judgment" (EPJ) in 1984. He recruited some 284 professionals and experts to analyze political and economic trends and events. Tetlock divided his target groups of forecasters into two distinguishable groups, hedgehogs and foxes.

Guess who had better forecasting results? Polymaths or career shapeshifters™ were able to forecast more accurate results. They were open to different options and possibilities, willing to learn more about each domain, and collected enough data across several domains and industries. On the other side, specialists and experts performed poorly in forecasting as a result of being focused on one big (single) idea, while ignoring all other possibilities. They looked at each problem from too narrow a perspective.

Career shapeshifters™ are capable of solving new and complicated problems more effectively than specialists. David Epstein, author of the bestseller *Range: Why Generalists Triumph in a Specialized World*, defines the big difference between a kind learning environment and a wicked learning environment. In a kind learning environment, people only need to repeat learning patterns until they master the major skills they need—think chess, golf, and firefighting. In such environments, the norm is to be highly specialized regarding what you did yesterday, are doing today, or will do tomorrow.

Myth #1 "You Need to Be a Supreme Specialist"

In today's world, wicked-complicated rules prevail. We face new problems every day in our day-to-day working and personal lives. Dealing with a wicked-complicated problem with a one-domain experience won't work. "Relying on one-single domain in a wicked-complicated world can be disastrous," Epstein noted.

Solving such complicated problems requires widening our horizons and using our experiences from other domains. It requires building analogical-thinking skills that bring an out-of-the-box-experience or a solution to your new domain from your old expertise. "Cross-domain analogical thinking" or "analogical reasoning" has been proved scientifically as one of the most effective techniques to generate innovative ideas and find solutions for new problems. Analogical reasoning is using an analogy, a type of comparison between two things, to develop understanding and meaning. It's commonly used to make decisions, solve problems, and communicate.

Shapeshifters™ are better able to solve complicated problems based on their previous experiences by using analogical reasoning.

Career shapeshifters™ are better leaders. In his book *How Will You Measure Your Life?* Harvard University professor Clayton M. Christensen said "management is the most noble of professions if it is practiced well. No other occupation offers as many ways to help others learn and grow, take responsibility, be recognized for achievement, and contribute to the success of a team." Christensen realized most of his MBA students were focused on buying, selling, and investing in companies, while being a leader requires using several skills at the same time. MBA graduates spend most of their lives focused on one specialty (that is, sales, marketing, product development, or finance). Only when they are in a position to be promoted do they realize they don't have other skills they will need, such as managing a team that specializes in another field, grasping knowledge about a new industry, or even making high-quality big decisions on behalf of their organization.[10]

In entrepreneurship, despite the widely-held belief that the most successful company CEOs are young and fresh out of grad school, the most successful start-ups have been founded by CEOs who were in their mid-forties. Research has also shown that the probability of a start-up's success rises with a CEO's age (at least until they are in their fifties) as well as the CEO's previous experiences.[11]

MY OWN EXPERIENCE WITH CAREER SHAPESHIFTING™

When I graduated from the faculty of Pharmacy, Cairo University and decided to change my career to diplomacy, I received lots of negative feedback and criticism from the people around me:

- "You are a pharmacist. What do you understand about diplomacy, politics, and economics?"

- "Are you stupid or what? You never can do that."

- "Be realistic and do what other graduates did. Do what you know how to do."

---

[10] Clayton M. Christensen, *How Will You Measure Your Life?* (Boston: Harvard Business Review Press), 2017.

[11] Pierre Azoulay, Benjamin F. Jones, J. Daniel Kim, and Javier, Miranda, "Research: The Average Age of a Successful Startup Founder is 45," *Harvard Business Review*, July 11, 2018, https://hbr.org/2018/07/research-the-average-age-of-a-successful-startup-founder-is-45.

Myth #1 "You Need to Be a Supreme Specialist"

- "Do you know how much you will lose when you leave your career?"

- "You will have to start from scratch and go down the hierarchical ladder again."

I didn't know how to respond. I used to think that those critiques were probably right. But even when it was hard for me to decide which path I should take, I followed my passion. This meant listening to my gut and allowing myself to follow the natural flow of what God might want from me—my life's purpose.

I followed my passion when I studied chemistry and became a pharmacist. I followed my passion again when I decided to become a diplomat, even though I was swimming against the current. I knew I was fulfilling my dreams and following my passion—that was enough for me.

What I didn't expect was how I was able to turn my weaknesses into strengths and learn new skills quickly and efficiently. When I transitioned again, this time into banking, I was surprised at how I was able to transfer and transform my skills to fit my new career. In fact, with every career transition, I have added new competencies to my growing pools of skills.

I had become a career shapeshifter™.

Now, as an entrepreneur, career coach, and author—while building my fifth career as a startup founder and app developer—I see the world from a completely different perspective. I see a world full of potential and opportunity. I have built more skills than I ever imagined I would, and am much more confident in myself as a result. The world from a polymath perspective is much more interesting and fun. You always have a bird's-eye view and see the bigger picture.

While I am running my business as a career and business coach, and writing my books and blog, I am able to learn other skills and integrate knowledge from seemingly unrelated experiences and careers. I still use my medical experience every single day in my personal life, while I am able to connect and advise some corporations on finding the right funding for their infrastructure projects in several developing countries. In my banking career I have been successful at bringing in hundreds of millions of dollars of infrastructure project financing to developing countries, including my native Egypt, where I was able to develop a business worth $1 billion.

I am also engaging in conversations that help companies operate in other cultural environments. I am an advocate (with other cultural experts) for building multicultural understanding in a multicultural and diverse context.

My point is that I am living a life that is much more interesting and fulfilling compared to the life I would have lived had I listened to people around me and stuck to my first career as a pharmacist. By following our passions, each of us has a chance to be his or her unique self and offer a unique value proposition to others.

If it's necessary that half the world needs to be comprised of specialists, then the other half must be polymaths or career shapeshifters™. *We need career shapeshifters™ as much as we need specialists. We need people who are able to connect domains together as much as we need people who are expert at one small area of specialization.*

We need career shapeshifters™ as much as we need specialists. We need people who are able to connect domains together as much as we need people who are expert at one small area of specialization.

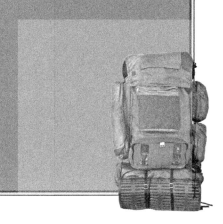

The choice should be *only* yours: not society's, not your boss, not your parents or friends. Live *your* dream, not someone else's. By being a career shapeshifter™, you will have more of a competitive edge than you realize. You will be your own unique and authentic version of yourself and not a cheap copy of someone else.

MYTH BUSTERS

1. Specialization is not the only definition of career success.

2. Polymathy has been rooted in history more than specialization. Many of the most influential people in history have been polymaths, also known as career shapeshifters™.

3. Becoming a polymath or career shapeshifter™ is the new way to succeed in a specialized world.

4. Career shapeshifting™ is essential to success—more freedom in crossing the borders between domains and careers is the future.

5. Cross-domain activities foster career success by building on previously learned skills.

MYTH #2

Change Is Too Risky

"The price of doing the same old thing is far higher

than the price of change."

— BILL CLINTON

The myth goes like this: Everyone should strive to have a stable life. People love stability, and hate change. No one likes surprises!

———◆———

Does this sound familiar? "I can't imagine how my life would change if I had to move. I can't leave my job and start from scratch somewhere else—I don't know what the repercussions of that change are. Change is risky and I can't handle that much risk in my life. What if I fail?"

But what if you *don't* fail?

PLAYING IT SAFE IS RISKY

When we are in our comfort zones, we fool ourselves into thinking there is no need to do more, and less is best. Our ability to learn diminishes because we get accustomed to living without change. That's why you need to be aware of the *comfort zone effect*. When you are too comfortable, you avoid exploring new challenges or pursuing your passions and dreams. Change scares you and keeps you static—or worse.

In reality, feeling as if you're not in your comfort zone is a good thing because it forces you to test your abilities and keep learning. Challenging yourself will elevate you to the next level. If you live your life without exploring new challenges, you will miss out on so much, including the opportunity to know yourself better. When you challenge yourself, you get to fully understand your capacity and potential. When you look at your life as a series of challenges, one after the other, life gets more rewarding and enjoyable as you meet those challenges.

When you are too comfortable, you can get disillusioned about your dreams because achieving those dreams means leaving your comfort zone. You may enjoy the sweetness of your comfort zone for a while, but that sweetness will eventually turn sour.

When you are stuck in your comfort zone, you never get the opportunity to find out what really matters to you—what your passions are, and what your life purpose is. Instead, you remain stuck in your daily routines, unable to pursue what is truly fulfilling.

When you are too comfortable,

you can get disillusioned about

your dreams because achieving

those dreams means leaving your

comfort zone. You may enjoy the

sweetness of your comfort zone for

a while, but that sweetness will

eventually turn sour.

Don't get me wrong—we all have routines, including me. But routines are only useful when they empower you to build positive habits. Otherwise, routines can turn you into a lazy and static version of yourself—the one who is unable to explore new things and learn more every day. That laziness is what kills your career and threatens to make you bitter.

"The Comfort Zone"

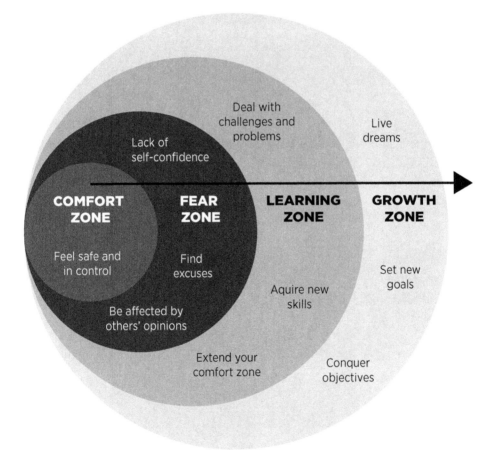

Deal with challenges and problems

Live dreams

Lack of self-confidence

COMFORT ZONE

FEAR ZONE

LEARNING ZONE

GROWTH ZONE

Feel safe and in control

Find excuses

Set new goals

Aquire new skills

Be affected by others' opinions

Extend your comfort zone

Conquer objectives

LEAVING YOUR COMFORT ZONE

Let's explore how the journey looks when you leave your comfort zone. It is crucial that you know in advance what you will face when you start taking your first steps toward the unknown. When you know what you are going to face, you build your own expectations for the kinds of challenges and obstacles you are going to face in each step, making you better prepared for what comes ahead. Let's look at each zone, as illustrated above.

Comfort Zone

When you are in your comfort zone, you are doing what you know. You get accustomed to what you are doing because you feel safe and in control of your own destiny—there's no pain. But staying too long in that zone will hinder your ability to learn new skills, grow, or adapt to any new environment or change. Therefore, once you feel you have accomplished a major project at work or in your personal life, and while you are celebrating your successes, you should also ask yourself this simple question: *"What's next?"* Ask yourself this question after each successful step in your career. Continuously making this inquiry will encourage you to get out of your comfort zone and into the next one, the *Fear Zone*.

Fear Zone

The daunting number of uncertainties and risks that you will encounter in the *fear zone* are what makes it so hard to leave your comfort zone. In this zone, critics will attack you. People will depict you as someone who traded a stable life and steady paycheck for an unknown future. To find a fulfilling career and enjoy what you are doing, you need to accept that some people spend more time putting their noses into other people's affairs than minding their own business. Paulo Coelho, author of *The Alchemist*, put it this way: "When you possess a treasure within you, and you want to tell people about it, seldom you are believed."

In this zone, you have less confidence in your abilities because of the challenges you are facing, but don't worry—this reaction is completely normal. If you are not sure of what you are doing, you'll gravitate back to your comfort zone. But, if you are persistent enough, you will soon move from the fear zone into the *learning zone*.

Learning Zone

Once you know how to manage and control your fears, you can (and will) start enjoying the learning process. Once you start experiencing what it is like to learn new things, both large and small, you will find it hard to go back to your comfort and fear zones. The more time you spend in your learning zone, the more certain you will be of the potential that is waiting for you on the other side. The more time and effort you spend on learning, the greater your ability to visualize future opportunities. It is very rewarding to learn something you never imagined learning.

Growth Zone

When you learn how to build your potential and acquire new skills, it will be obvious that this is what you were created to do. You will be able to face new challenges and conquer them. The growth zone is where you actually start achieving your goals and realize your life's purpose—what you were born to do. It is where you are able to widen your horizons and build the skills that make you the most valuable asset that you can invest in.

CHANGE AS A CONSTANT

Very little is guaranteed in life. The idea of specializing in one career or working in one organization until you retire has become an outdated concept, if not extinct. Look at how the COVID-19 pandemic that started in 2020 impacted the lives of millions of people and businesses across the globe within a very short span of time. *Like it or not, even if you accept a static life and remain in your comfort zone, that static life might not last for you, because the world is constantly moving and shifting.*

Change happens whether you like it or not—that's why it is so important to predict it, prepare for it, and embrace it as best we can.

Change Over Time

Do our personality traits change over time? Are we the same people we were ten years ago? Do we stay unchanged? To answer these questions, psychologist Dan Gilbert and his team measured the personalities, values, and preferences of more than nineteen thousand people who ranged in age from eighteen to sixty-eight and asked them to report how much they had changed over the past decade and/or to predict how much they would change in the next decade.[12]

The results were astonishing. Young, middle-aged, and older people all believed they had changed a lot in the past compared

---

[12] Jordi Quoidbach, Daniel T. Gilbert, and Timothy D. Wilson, "The End of History Illusion," *Science* 339:6115 (January 2013), https://www.researchgate.net/publication/234047936_The_End_of_History_Illusion&sa=D&source=docs&ust=1656351031574732&usg=AOvVaw0DT6Pms3p-e9PXG4Ec0hA6.

Like it or not, even if you accept a static life and remain in your comfort zone, that static life might not last for you, because the world is constantly moving and shifting.

Change happens whether you like it or not—that's why it is so important to predict it, prepare for it, and embrace it as best we can.

to the present. They also mostly reported that they had become the person who will stay unchanged for the rest of their lives, and that they would change less in the future compared to the past. What the majority of participants could not explain was why their personalities changed in the past, and why they expected not to change much in the future.

One possible explanation was that people have a fundamental misconception about how they will look in the future. Time is a powerful force that transforms people's preferences, and reshapes their passions and values, not to mention the way they think. Time has a powerful effect that can alter your entire personality. Gilbert and his team called this effect "end of history illusion" and described it as the inability to understand the magnitude of changes that happen to us over time. We always underestimate that power of change on us when it comes to the future.

So even if you don't like change or are afraid of it, you will change and need to change because that is how we are wired. The fact is, humans are beings who are constantly changing.

MY OWN OBSESSION FOR CHANGE

Change has always been scary, especially for an introverted guy like me. As a kid, I was not naturally brave or extroverted. I had difficulty dealing with changes, big or small. Some classmates even described me as the most traditional, typical, and unchangeable boy in my high school.

Even so, I have always dreamed, including about having several careers. I knew I was shy, and had self-doubts, my own limiting beliefs, and feelings of being underestimated and underrated by

So even if you don't like change or are

afraid of it, you will change and need

to change because that is how we are

wired. The fact is, humans are beings

who are constantly changing.

Myth #2 Change Is Too Risky

others—all of which were working against me. But I also knew that hard work, persistence, and consistency could work for me. When I was twelve, I liked the idea of being a diplomat, and was lucky enough to have met a veteran diplomat (Ambassador Mohamed Fathy Elshazly, may he RIP) two years earlier who inspired me to follow this path. However, when I was sixteen, my passion suddenly changed to chemistry, and loving chemistry meant I had to be a pharmacist, a big change in my plans. I asked myself if I should pursue my old dream to be a diplomat, or should I follow the passion I have right now. At the same time, I wasn't interested in studying political and economic theories, but I enjoyed studying chemistry. I told my family that I could study chemistry now and still be able to apply for the diplomacy national competition after I graduated if I still had passion for it. So, I chose the former, and decided to study chemistry, for now. Following my passion was enough at that point in my life. I spent enough time on my passion—at that time, chemistry—that it was an easy decision.

"If I enjoy it for a few more years, why not?" I said to myself. Seven years later, when I was graduating, my passion shifted again. I enjoyed learning about chemistry for five years and satisfied that passion. But I also wondered, "Do I want to be a pharmacist for life? Or should I pursue my old dream to be a diplomat?"

It sounded scary at the time because it was such a big change and looked so insurmountable. But I didn't dwell on that. Instead, I spent more time on trying to understand my passion and deciding whether I saw myself as a pharmacist or a diplomat. I spent a year and a half trying to decide what I should do next, while working as a pharmacist.

I learned to make big decisions in my life during times when I feel the most spiritual—for me, that means during Ramadan, when I feel particularly close to God. In this instance, by the end of that period, I was able to make the decision that being a pharmacist was not what I was passionate about—I wanted to be a diplomat. In that role, I would have a chance to represent my country and my culture in the best way. I would be able to travel the world, while learning other languages and experiencing other cultures. I would be able to focus on myself and build my skills while working for my country—I determined that this was an ideal life for me.

My inner voice kicked in. "This is a big change. Aren't you afraid of that big change? Aren't you afraid of failure? You will have to compete with more than two thousand candidates; most of them are probably more experienced than you. Do you think you can make the cut to be one of thirty new diplomats, out of more than two thousand candidates? What will other people say when you tell them about your plans? They will laugh at you. Don't be ridiculous. This is your comfort zone. Don't leave it."

But by that time, I had already made up my mind, so I was able to reply firmly to that discouraging inner voice. "Yeah, I know all of that. But this is my dream. And this is the future life that I want to live. I don't want to be a pharmacist all my life. I want to be a diplomat and travel the world. Even if I fail, I have to try, because this is my passion now and I don't have anything to lose."

That was the conversation I had with myself every single day once I made my decision. But what made it easier to finally leave my comfort zone was spending enough time focused on understanding my passion and what it meant *to me*. I decided that I had to pursue it no matter how afraid I was. And I kept repeating this message every single day for another three years, until I did make it and was one of the thirty new diplomats.

This thinking helped me to become less sensitive and less resistant toward change. If I didn't embrace change, I would still be stuck in my comfort zone or what I can see now as "my old prison." Instead, by embracing change, I was able to grow, learn, and experience many things in my new professions, beyond what I used to know. I was able to conquer my fear of change. And when the winds of change visited me again, I was able to ride those winds, despite all the doubts I had and the challenges I faced. Each experience transformed me, and taught me that if I did it once, I could do it again.

My rule of thumb is that if my passions shift, I should shift with them. And if I sense a big change happening, I should pay attention. *When you build the capacity to accommodate, even welcome, change in your life, you can go even further and actually start predicting change. And by predicting change, you can proactively act on that change before it happens.*

Of course, now I can claim that change was the best thing that happened in my life. If I never pursued my passions or tried to go out of my comfort zone, I would still be regretting it. I am glad that I got out of my comfort zone because it changed my life.

Several years ago, while I was going through a difficult period of pressure and change at work, a friend asked me, "Do you know the difference between a precious stone and a normal (less valuable) one?" I responded that I didn't. "It is the pressure and the changes that the stone has been through over the years. The

When you build the capacity to

accommodate, even welcome, change

in your life, you can go even further

and actually start predicting change.

And by predicting change, you can

proactively act on that change before

it happens.

change in pressure is what makes the difference. The precious stone is underneath the ground experiencing extreme changes, including high pressure and heat. The normal stone didn't go through the same changes the precious stone did. We pay more for the precious stone because we know and appreciate the change it has gone through. The same applies to people: when changes occur because you are under pressure, you become a stronger, more precious soul. You shine and even thrive. On the contrary, if you don't go through that necessary pressure and suffering, forget it. You will live and die without adding any value to the world. The world will not notice whether you are alive or dead." Of course, too much pressure and change can be destructive to both your mental and physical health, so you need to understand what your limitations are. The point is that you should not choose to be static because you are afraid of change. With the right risks come big opportunities.

MYTH BUSTERS

1. Your comfort zone has a negative impact on your ability to learn new skills. Once you figure out that you are comfortable and nothing needs to change, it's time for a change.

2. Fear of the unknown is a major source of distraction and impacts your ability to make big decisions, big moves, and plan for big achievements in your life.

3. The only constant in life is change. Change happens to our personalities, our passions, our priorities, our values, and

our vision for life. If change is coming regardless, it is better to be prepared for it before it comes than to be unprepared when it arrives.

4. Life is about the journey, not the destination. We don't have a "must" destination in our lives. Like the best trips, be flexible with your itinerary, and enjoy the ride.

5. We are ever-changing creatures, so expect change, embrace it, learn to predict it, and even befriend it.

6. Make your change a transformation. Transformation is big, positive, revolutionary, and life-changing.

MYTH #3

It Is Too Late to Find Your
Dream Career

"People are capable, at any time in their lives, of doing what they dream of."

— PAULO COELHO,

AUTHOR OF THE ALCHEMIST

The myth goes like this: It's too late to make a big change and achieve my dreams. It is too late to change. I am too old for this. It's too late to go back to school and learn something new. I am too invested in what I'm doing to change my career. It is too late and risky to start a business at this point in my life.

Sound familiar? I can't tell you how many times I have heard this. As you know from earlier in this book, I've even had these own thoughts myself. I've heard this from people in their fifties and sixties, but also from people in their thirties and forties. When I was a pharmacist, I even heard these same words from my sixteen-year-old assistant. He had dropped out of school a few years earlier, and I was trying to convince him to go back and finish his studies.

My point is that pursuing what you are passionate about isn't about age at all. It is about attitude. I tried to convince my assistant to go back to school while still keeping his job. He started looking into his options again, but I left to embark on my diplomacy career before he made a decision. In the back of my mind, I always thought it would be tough for him to leave what he was doing because he was surrounded by people who discouraged him. Fast-forward sixteen years later, the coincidence led me to pass by the place where I used to work with him from 2003 to 2006 and I was not sure whom would be still working there from the old staff. To my surprise, the sixteen-year-old assistant is still working there. Now he is thirty-two years old, married with kids, but he could not go back to school. He was not able to change his life to the one he dreamed. He listened to the discouraging environment surrounding him and he could not ever change. I saw a sad smile on his face that he could not hide. As if he were saying to me, "Well, I could not pursue my dreams. I failed." So sad!

The last time I saw him I told him, "Mahmoud, study what is important for your future. And remember, you can never continue on your journey by sticking with the wrong company. Choose a new company, one with people who encourage each other to grow."

When I decided to go back to school and get my MBA, I met Dave, a sixty-eight-year-old accountant from the UK, who had also decided to get his MBA—he told me he wanted to acquire new skills and adapt to changing market demands. Even though they were at opposite ends regarding age, what really differentiated

Myth #3 It Is Too Late to Find Your Dream Career

Dave from Mahmoud was his *mindset*. Even though Mahmoud was much younger, Dave had more energy and curiosity. I asked Dave why he decided to pursue his MBA at this point in his life, given that it can take up to four years to complete the program; here's what he told me: "I am an accountant in a high school, and I would like to acquire more skills especially in marketing and operations, because I have a better chance to grow in my job and have more responsibility than I have now. I am also considering a career change, so this MBA might give me the opportunity to figure out a new path." His answer took me by surprise, and inspired me.

I wanted to observe Dave during our classes, because I was wondering how active and engaged he would be—would he rely more on younger colleagues to get things done without having to exert as much individual effort? I couldn't have been more wrong! Dave ended up being the most active person in his group. Like the rest of us, he stayed late to work on his team presentation—Dave was all in. On the day we presented, his performance was amazing. He delivered one of the best presentations I have ever seen. I felt like he was giving it everything he had—all the wisdom he has gathered over the years, combined with the confidence of someone with more than forty-five years of experience. Dave outshone his younger peers and, in the process, taught me a valuable lesson about my own assumptions.

On that day, I learned a big lesson that has stuck with me: *It is never too late to achieve your dreams. As long as you are breathing, there is no reason to stop yourself from pursuing your dreams, even if that means going back to school and starting a completely new career.*

It is never too late to achieve your dreams. As long as you are breathing, there is no reason to stop yourself from pursuing your dreams, even if that means going back to school and starting a completely new career.

If you didn't at least try, you will always regret it and wonder what you missed out on.

Thanks, Dave, for the inspiration!

Life is full of stories of people who changed their lives regardless of how old they were. For these folks, it didn't matter whether they started that process early in life or when they were in their fifties or sixties. What mattered was that they took action: they started when they felt they were ready for that change, even if it was after they retired.

BREAKING THE "IT'S TOO LATE MYTH"

When I interviewed her, Mary was in her sixties. Originally from Venezuela, she has lived most of her life in Miami. Mary is a great example of a devoted and motivated single mother. She earned her bachelor's degree in interior design and started her career working in a small design company in Miami. Things were looking good for Mary: she got married, had a good job, and three terrific kids. What else would anybody want? But deep inside, Mary was not fulfilled. Neither her marriage nor her work were satisfying her, despite her relentless efforts to make them work.

After Mary's epiphany that she wasn't happy, she made two life-changing decisions around the same time: the first was to separate from her husband, and the second was to start her own business by opening a small furniture shop. When we spoke, Mary told me: "Leaving both was a hard choice, but I knew it was the right thing for me. I had to set myself free and start another new life where everything around me looked new and fresh. I was patient because of my kids: my oldest was twelve, my younger was four by that time and I could not hold on anymore."

Life is full of stories of people who changed their lives regardless of how old they were. For these folks, it didn't matter whether they started that process early in life or when they were in their fifties or sixties. What mattered was that they took action: they started when they felt they were ready for that change, even if it was after they retired.

Myth #3 It Is Too Late to Find Your Dream Career

"After my divorce I started working in a big showroom as a designer in sales." Mary did really well until they closed the showroom and she decided to open a design studio, that soon evolved into a furniture store.

She told me, "By the time I started my new business I was already married for the second time."

It was very challenging in the beginning because money was tight, but as the old expression goes, "where there is a will, there is a way." Her ex-boss opened a new furniture showroom and after nine months of opening he offered Mary to buy the store, even helped her finance the new store, and soon thereafter things started taking off. She built a career based on her previous experience as an interior designer and built a business she was passionate about. Even though the people around her felt her decision was risky, Mary never second-guessed herself. She knew she was making the right decision by following her passion.

Fast-forward a few years, and things have never been better. Her kids are on their own, building their own lives and families, and her business is thriving. Mary was developing an international client base, as well as a presence in other markets.

"But sometimes life brings you even more surprises. And I mean bad surprises. In 2010 I was diagnosed with breast cancer and a long way of suffering had just started," Mary told me. "I don't know how I built such courage to face it. But believe it or not, I brought in the entire family and told them that I had breast cancer and that it was time to allocate my wealth to each one of them. I even allocated money to my granddaughters."

Mary started a tough chemotherapy journey that went through both 2010 and 2011. It was indeed a journey of pain and suffering: the physical (and emotional) effects of chemotherapy, the financial burden of her treatment, and the decline in her business as a result of her illness: "The decline in my business was predictable because of the medical costs, inability to focus as much on my business because of my sickness, and the added challenge of a financial crisis that affected most businesses in the U.S. at that time."

But the good news is that Mary has recovered. She went through her experience with the support and help of her family, friends, and clients—she managed to not only survive but came out of her experience much stronger than before.

When I asked Mary if she thought she would survive this ordeal, she told me: "All I knew at that time was that I would have to face it all with courage: face disease with courage; continue fighting for my family and business. I even expected myself to face death with courage if I had to." I asked Mary what her secret was that got her through the dark times, and she responded with a one-word answer—faith—and explained what she meant: "It was faith that got me through and helped me survive all of this with the hope that I could make it to the other side safe and sound. I knew I didn't have anything to lose, because I have always done my best for the people around me. I have done my best for my family and for my business, so why regret—or even have anything to regret." I asked Mary how she managed to build the faith that saw her through her ordeal:

It is not a one-day event or a linear process. You learn to build faith through life, by going through tough experiences, by getting tested and continuously pushing your boundaries.

"It is not a one-day event or a linear process. You learn to build faith through life, by going through tough experiences, by getting tested and continuously pushing your boundaries.

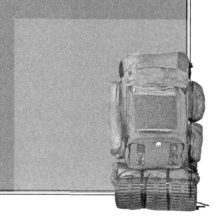

"When my son was two months old, our doctor told us that he suffered from congenital hydrocephalus, a buildup of excess cerebral fluid in the brain at birth," Mary said. "The extra fluid could increase pressure on my son's brain, which would cause imbalance in movement, brain damage, and mental and physical problems. The doctor mentioned there is less than a 5 percent possibility that my kid would recover, and because recovery is so rare, doesn't count on it. But I never lost hope that my son would recover. I took a year off work and just focused on him. I followed up with several doctors and never lost hope. I believed there was always a chance if I did my best. I prayed a lot that my kid would recover and live his life as a normal person. And destiny lent a hand. One day we were all on a boat trip and I saw my one-year-old kid trying to keep his balance. At that moment, I knew that he would make it. This was a big test of my faith and I always remind myself of that experience when things turn bad. I always say things will be alright. The one who took care of us in those situations will take care of us through any other hardship, and this is what made it easier for me to survive my cancer, family, and business hardships."

In 2015 she got a divorce from her second husband after eighteen years together. What came next was unexpected and took me by surprise. Although Mary's business took off again, she decided to close it. When she told her son that she had decided to close the family business, he said, "No, Mum, I will join you again in the business. Don't close it." He said this, thinking she was tired of working by herself, but what he didn't know was that the passion she had for her business had been replaced by another. *Sometimes we don't realize that our passions change or shift, and that we need to address that shift, or risk losing track of what is important and fulfilling to us.* And this is exactly what happened to Mary: she started to lose her passion for her business.

During her sickness, Mary looked for inspiration from different sources to help her build a strong and resilient mindset in order to mentally survive her sickness. She started reading Brian Weiss' books including *Through Time into Healing* and *Miracles Happen*, before moving on to Tony Robbins' books and courses. Since then, she has never stopped growing her mindset and learning new things. She even got a certificate in hypnotherapy. She is a John Maxwell-certified coach as well as an NLP New Code practitioner.

Even with all the difficulties she went through, that period was so powerful it caused her to reshape her thinking and become even more resilient. Over the course of her life, Mary noticed that most of the women she knew who were at least fifty years old had stopped enjoying their lives and given up on their dreams, including her mother—Mary wanted to avoid that fate: "That idea of living your life without enjoying or dreaming after a certain age was so scary to me. I have seen my mother not able to do so and I never wanted to repeat that in my life; this gave me another purpose to my life. With all the hardships I have faced and the strong mindset that I built to face all of this, I saw my new passion leading me to start a coaching business to empower women over fifty to continue dreaming about their lives and never stop living."

Mary was wise enough to recognize that her passions were shifting—from her former interior design business to her new coaching business. She knew that she could bring value to what she wanted to do, as someone other women could relate to. She

Sometimes we don't realize that our passions change or shift, and that we need to address that shift, or risk losing track of what is important and fulfilling to us.

had been through similar tough situations others had experienced, from seeing her marriage end, to surviving cancer, to supporting her family, to building her business and then rebuilding it again. Someone else may have responded with defeat: "OK. I am done. I have had enough of life and its hardships, and it is time for me to relax and do nothing." Instead, Mary took the opposite approach. She saw another opportunity to start a new career in her mid-sixties and do something that would positively impact other people by giving them hope. She saw an opportunity to enjoy another passion, build another passion project, and feed her life's purpose. In fact, Mary has found another new passion: writing. And without much preparation or training, she started writing about things that she liked. By the time we had our interview, Mary had already written three books, two on personal growth and one about her journey of surviving cancer.

We need more people like Dave and Mary. It's worth repeating: it's never too late to pursue your passions, to achieve your life dreams, to learn the skills that you always wanted to learn, to embark on the adventures that you always wanted to take, and to travel to the destinations that you always dreamed about. This is the secret to living a fulfilled and a regret-free life. Start where you are. Start now and don't think too much about the result or whether you have the time to achieve the result you want. A big part of enjoying life is *pursuing* the things you like before actually *achieving* them. Most high achievers and successful people recall their early days of hard work pursuing their dreams fondly, even as their best days ever. So, remember that hope is what brings things closer to reality. You need to be consistent in your efforts to make things happen—and you need time to achieve them. Pray that you get enough time to get what you want, and get started sooner rather than later. *Tempus fugit*! Time flies!

WHAT DOES RESEARCH TELL US ABOUT AGE?

Research doesn't support the assumptions that most of us have: If you could not achieve career success in your twenties; if you haven't amassed wealth in your thirties; if you haven't built your unicorn by the time you're forty, you'll never be successful. You'll never achieve your dreams or be able to follow your passions. *Life is full of stories about "late bloomers" who defied the odds.*

Studies show that the average age of Fortune 500 CEOs rose sharply to fifty-eight years old in 2019 compared to fifty-four years old in 2018. In fact, the average age of Fortune 500 chief executives is fifty-seven.[13] Also, the number of S&P 500 CEOs in their forties has declined sharply in the past decade.[14] Even in the small business market, 57 percent of small business owners surveyed by Guidant Financial were older than fifty, a small increase year over year. All

---

[13] Allana Akhtar, "Corporate America is Seeing a Spike in the Age of CEOs Being Hired – and Yes, They're Overwhelmingly White Men," Business Insider India, Nov. 1, 2019, https://www.businessinsider.in/strategy/news/corporate-america-is-seeing-a-spike-in-the-age-of-ceos-being-hired-and-yes-theyre-overwhelmingly-white-men/articleshow/71856494.cms10#:~:text=A%202019%20report%20from%20the,54%20between%202018%20and%202019.

[14] Chip Cutter, "CEOs Under 50 Are a Rare Find in the S&P 500," *The Wall Street Journal*, updated May 22, 2019, https://www.wsj.com/articles/ceos-under-50-are-a-rare-find-in-the-s-p-500-11558517401.

Life is full of stories

about "late bloomers" who

defied the odds.

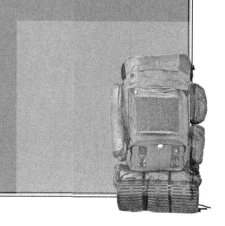

of this supported a phenomenon that is called "aging CEOs."[15]

There are several reasons why, but for purposes of our discussion, we'll focus on this one: these CEOs reflect a combination of compounded wisdom and multiple experiences acquired over the course of a career when compared to someone with less experience. In fact, it is rare to find a Fortune 500 CEO who is younger than fifty.

Another report showed that more C-suite executives than ever are in their seventies.[16] The reports detail both the challenges and opportunities that these executives bring to their organizations, but the message is:

When you grow older, there are more opportunities for you than what you may think, because you grow with your experiences.

The Late Achiever's Phenomenon

In their book, *Dark Horse: Achieving Successes Through The Pursuit of Fulfillment*, authors Todd Rose and Ogi Ogas studied the reasons behind the extraordinary success of women and men who achieved impressive success late in their careers, despite the fact that nobody around them saw that success happening.

One of the main reasons for this was that those late achievers ignored the destination and kept exploring their journeys in their own ways. Even if they started their careers picking a destination strategy, they changed their strategy over time to refocus more on the journey of fulfilling their passions and exploring their inner-

---

[15] Jane Johnson, "70 Is the New 50: Aging CEOs Provide Both Opportunities and Challenges for Businesses," Business Transition Academy, June 12, 2019, https://www.businesstransitionacademy.com/strategic-business-planning-blog/70-is-the-new-50-aging-ceos-provide-both-opportunities-and-challenges-for-businesses.
[16] Ibid.

When you grow older, there are

more opportunities for you than what

you may think, because you grow

with your experiences.

selves rather than picking a destination and sticking to it no matter what happened. This strategy of "choosing no strategy" or "no destination" might take longer than average to achieve, but it has the power to help you to excel in your own unique way (that is, on your own terms) and to find your own unique and unconventional approach to doing things.

The question shouldn't be, "how long do I need to master this skill?"—it should be, "is this the right strategy for me to learn this skill?" Focus less on how long the journey will take, and more time on ensuring you are on the *right* journey.

MYTH BUSTERS

1. It's never too late to pursue your dreams, even dreams from your childhood.

2. The biggest and longest-lasting regrets are not the ones that come from our mistakes—they are the ones that come from the dreams we wanted to pursue but never did.

3. Time is relative: take your time and do what you love to do.

4. As you grow older, there are more opportunities for you than you may realize because with each experience you grow.

5. High achievers focus on the journey, not the destination.

MYTH #4

You Have Bills to Pay

"You are not here in this life to pay your bills and die."

— U N K N O W N

The myth goes like this: I have bills to pay. I have responsibilities and have to take care of my family. I'm too busy taking care of my family to even think about achieving those big dreams.

———•———

If this sounds like you, you need to ask yourself: What is your life's purpose? To earn enough money to pay your bills? To simply eat, drink, and die? There's a reason why many lottery winners report being unhappy and disappointed, even though they are financially set for life.

Do you feel that your life has meaning? Are you helping other people, or are you only focused on yourself? Are you an advocate for something bigger? Do you seek values such as equality, freedom, or fighting climate change?

MASLOW'S HIERARCHY OF NEEDS

Self-actualization
Desire to accomplish everything that one can, to become the most that one can be

Esteem needs
Self-confidence and independence, respect and acknowledgment from others

Love and belonging
Friendships, family, social groups, community, intimacy

Safety needs
Protection, stability and well-being, health and financial security

Physiological needs
Food, water, breathing, homeostasis, sexual reproduction

The psychologist Abraham Maslow created a hierarchy of needs, a five-stage model that is built as a pyramid. The model suggests that people are motivated to achieve certain needs and that some needs take precedence over others. The bottom of the pyramid, physical survival, is our most basic need and the first thing that motivates our behavior. Physical survival supports the other four levels of the pyramid. Each level above that represents the next level of motivation. Let's take a closer look.

Level One: Physiological Needs

These are needs required for our survival—they are generally not negotiable and include things like air, food, drink, shelter, clothing, warmth, sex, and sleep. If these needs are not satisfied the human body cannot function optimally, and we may die. Maslow considered physiological needs the most important because all other needs become secondary until these needs are met.

Level Two: Safety Needs

Once an individual's physiological needs are satisfied, the need for security and safety become very important. We have a need for order, predictability, and control in our lives. These needs can be fulfilled by both family and society (that is, police, schools, business, medical care). Examples of Level Two include emotional security, financial security, freedom from fear, social stability, and well-being.

Level Three: Love and Belonging Needs

After physiological and safety needs have been fulfilled, the third level of the pyramid is social and involves feelings of belonging. In this case, "belonging" refers to our emotional needs for interpersonal relationships, feeling connected to others, and being part of a group.

Level Four: Esteem Needs

This level of the pyramid deals with self-worth, accomplishment, and respect. Maslow classified esteem needs into two categories: (1) esteem for oneself (dignity, achievement, mastery, independence) and (2) the desire for reputation or respect from others (status, prestige).

Level Five: Self-actualization Needs

The needs at the top of the pyramid refer to the realization of an individual's potential, self-fulfillment, personal growth, and peak experiences. Maslow describes this level as the desire to accomplish everything that one can; to become the most that one can become. Self-actualization represents the pinnacle to what we have worked towards over the course of our lives.

To live a fulfilled and successful life, we need to fulfill the needs represented in these five levels—or at least have some balance among all of them. How can we achieve this?

Once you fulfill the basic but essential needs in Level One (having enough food to eat and a place to live), you can move to each of the subsequent four levels until you reach the peak.

Back to the "you have bills to pay" myth: where do you think paying your bills shows up in this pyramid? If you said the first (base) level, you are correct—you need to pay bills to survive. Think about this: Do you really want to spend your entire life at the bottom of the pyramid, and miss out on a potentially amazing and extraordinary life at the pyramid's apex? Why spend your life at the bottom of the pyramid and not be able to see the view from the top?

YOUR ZONE OF GENIUS

Self-actualization and living a fulfilled life is about identifying your dreams and pursuing them. It is about knowing your life's purpose and going after it. It is about knowing what your unique gifts and value are, and how you can share that value with the world. It is about knowing your "zone of genius" and using it to change people's lives around you.

Each of us has a zone of genius. *Your zone of genius is when you are at your best, doing what you are the best at, fully enjoying your work and what you are doing, and there is no one who can compete with you in this zone.* Having a zone of genius doesn't require some predisposition to greatness—you don't have to be a born genius or a member of Mensa. But you do need to look within yourself.

Your zone of genius is when

you are at your best, doing what you

are the best at, fully enjoying your

work and what you are doing, and

there is no one who can compete with

you in this zone.

Your zone of genius might be in painting, soccer, being a doctor or engineer. It really doesn't matter what your zone of genius is, but the first rule for *finding* it is to follow your passions. Your zone of genius may even change over time. Some people may have multiple zones of genius; they often pursue several passions and transition from one career to another. *Living your life's purpose is the highest level you can aspire to, and it begins with following your passions.*

Don't get me wrong, we all have responsibilities and families we need to take care of. Remember, we can't build a pyramid without a strong base. But that doesn't mean we can't also pursue our dreams. It makes sense that you might work for an organization or in a career that you don't especially enjoy temporarily so you can cover your expenses. But you should *never* ignore or forget your dreams. You may move up and down those five levels of Maslow's pyramid, trying your best to satisfy your needs—but you can't spend your entire life stuck at the first or second levels, expecting that you will also enjoy a fulfilled and purposeful life. Each of us has a purpose in life; each of us needs to figure out how to realize that purpose.

MY OWN "YOU HAVE BILLS TO PAY" STORY

When I was sixteen, it was a scary decision to have to choose one major and one specialization, knowing that these choices would impact me for the rest of my life—whatever vocation I chose, I would spend a lifetime in it. I used to ask myself over and over, "How do I know if this is the right fit for me?" Have you ever been in a situation where you had to make a decision and became paralyzed with fear, constantly second-guessing yourself? Trying to sort things out can be confusing and daunting. When I was faced with making that decision, I was incredibly confused because I had many dreams: I wanted to be a soccer player, an astronaut, a diplomat, an engineer, a musician, a chemist, and sometimes even a singer.

I decided to stick with what I felt was my biggest passion that time, chemistry. As a teenager, I was interested in studying all types of chemistry, and pharmacy allowed me to do that. Did I want to be a pharmacist? I didn't know for sure, but doubts managed to creep in. I dreamed of being an astronaut when I was six years old, but then realized it might be hard to achieve in my home country. I dreamed of being a soccer player, but that was derailed after I got a serious knee injury when I was fourteen years old. Diplomacy was still one of my big dreams that felt achievable, but I wasn't ready to commit to studying political theory.

I was stuck with my pharmaceutical studies for five years, even though I wasn't entirely convinced I would become a pharmacist. I rationalized my decision by telling myself I would study something that I loved for five years, and then go from there. By the time I graduated, however, I was already sure that being a pharmacist was not for me. I was glad that I satisfied one of my passions by studying chemistry, but I knew that it wasn't something I wanted to do for the rest of my life.

That was when I started looking inside myself again, searching to find my next passion—diplomacy. I took some time to make my decision because I wanted to give it all that I had. I didn't want to go down a path only to realize later it wasn't right for me. I imagined myself in my new career as a diplomat. I saw myself traveling the world, speaking different languages, having friends and colleagues

Can you imagine being stuck

your entire life in a career that

doesn't fulfill you, just because

you were afraid of not being able

to pay your bills?

Myth #4 You Have Bills to Pay

from across the globe and with different cultural backgrounds. I saw that this new career could fulfill my passions for travel, representing my country, and helping to bring more understanding among cultures. I meditated and prayed for guidance from God and the universe to make sure I was making the right choice, and that I was ready.

As I shared with you earlier, my choice was not met with enthusiasm. When I shared my decision with people around me including my manager, colleagues, friends, and family, almost all of them told me I was wasting my time and my life. I received discouraging messages every single day for more than three years, as I continued to work as a pharmacist while preparing for the diplomacy exam. Once my boss said to me, "Don't you see that your friends are better off than you? They have more money than you do. They own their own homes and you don't. They have cars and you don't." You know what? I wasn't deterred. Here's how I responded: "Good for them. I am happy for them, but I am not here to pay my bills and then die. I am fine with not having all the things they have because I really want to achieve this dream. It is everything for me now."

Being a pharmacist paid well and could have provided me with financial stability, but it didn't offer me the lifestyle that I wanted to live. It was a good job that I enjoyed and would appreciate for as long as I was there, but I knew I couldn't stay there forever. And you know what? I am so glad that I made the decision I did! *Can you imagine being stuck your entire life in a career that doesn't fulfill you, just because you were afraid of not being able to pay your bills?* This is not the life I wish for myself—or anyone else for that matter.

If I didn't make the choices I made, I would have missed out on a once-in-a-lifetime opportunity. Instead, I realized that I had options: I could do more interesting things in life and not feel stuck in a rut. It's hard to change careers, but it's not impossible. The hardships I encountered in every career transition I made have helped me pivot successfully and has empowered me to help others realize their passions, and then fight for and achieve their dreams. These experiences and challenges have resulted in an extraordinary life, despite the challenges (maybe even because of them).

How about you? Are you stuck in a career that you hate just because you have bills to pay? If so, you are missing a golden opportunity to know how amazing you can be. I am not asking you to jump off a cliff. Instead, I'm telling you not to ignore your passions. Give yourself the time to understand these new passions and devise an exit plan, while you are still able to pay your bills.

Devising that plan is not as difficult as you might think. You can still make plans while continuing to work where you are, enabling you to pay your bills.

MYTH BUSTERS

1. Your purpose in life is bigger than paying your bills.

2. While you pay your bills and take care of your financial responsibilities, ask yourself what your life's purpose is. By exploring and pursuing your passions, you will discover your purpose.

3. You don't need to take big leaps. Instead, give yourself the time you need to make a transition when the time is right.

4. We all should fulfill the five levels of needs in Maslow's pyramid, or at least have some measure of balance among

them so we can live fulfilled and successful lives. The ultimate goal is to be able to see the view from the top of the pyramid.

MYTH #5

Focus on Your Strengths, Not Your Weaknesses

"Unsuccessful people find their strengths and spend their lives making their strengths stronger, often ignoring their weaknesses, until one day their weaknesses cannot be ignored anymore. Successful people find their weaknesses and make them strengths."

— ROBERT KIYOSAKI

The myth goes like this: It is easier to work on your strengths, rather than your weaknesses. Making your strengths stronger is easier than strengthening your weaknesses.

Conventional wisdom tells us that successful people focus on their strengths, while pretty much ignoring their weaknesses. If you want to win—and win fast—you can't afford to waste time working on your weaknesses. Conventional wisdom also tells us that when you focus on your strengths, you grow them more, but if you devote energy to strengthening your weaknesses, you will get mired down in mediocrity and never excel.

What do you think? Sounds like pretty typical advice from career experts, doesn't it? Kind of makes sense, don't you think?

But what if your strengths don't align with your passions? What if you are already bored with your strengths, and feel as if you are doing the same thing every day? What if you want to learn something new—something you never tried before? What if you find out that you have passion for something you never imagined doing? Isn't doing something completely new a weakness because you aren't focusing on what you already know (that is, your strengths)?

MY OWN "FOCUS ON YOUR STRENGTHS, NOT YOUR WEAKNESSES" STORY

I was an introverted child, so it took me awhile to make friends. As a teenager, I focused on doing things I do by myself: reading, listening to music, singing by myself. I considered myself the shyest kid in my school.

After becoming a pharmacist, I was still introverted and shy. That changed when I decided to pursue a career as a diplomat. I was passionate about wanting to represent my country and my culture in the best way possible. But to me, being introverted was a big weakness because it held me back—I was uncomfortable communicating with others. Obviously, to be a successful diplomat, you had to be comfortable communicating with other people, often from different cultures and in different languages.

Myth #5 Focus On Your Strengths, Not Your Weaknesses

It didn't help that people discouraged me: "You are a pharmacist. You don't know anything about diplomacy, politics, and economics. And on top of all of that, you are an introvert. How can you be a diplomat? You should continue doing what you are already good at."

I already knew it would be hard to change my career to a new one that I had no experience or training in. But I also knew that it was what I had my heart set on doing. I used that passion to my advantage—it kept me focused on my goal.

I ended up being right, and my naysayers wrong. As you already know, my passion made it possible for me to achieve my goal and become a diplomat. After studying to qualify as a diplomat while still earning a living as a pharmacist, I was chosen as one of thirty new diplomats out of almost two thousand applicants. I credit my passion for making that possible.

Fast-forward ten years. I was a successful diplomat with a reputation as someone able to build a network quickly and efficiently. To my surprise, some people who never knew me before I was a diplomat thought that I was born as one because they saw how I had mastered my profession. Even when I mastered my diplomacy profession, I never thought that seizing a small opportunity (being the focal point of all the Chinese outbound infrastructure projects in my country) was the gateway to my new banking career. The big opportunity sends you smaller opportunities before it knocks on your door. The only way to seize that big opportunity is by acting on the smaller ones.

Spending my entire day on

something I don't have a passion for,

even if it is a strength, is not the

right answer—for me or you.

Myth #5 Focus On Your Strengths, Not Your Weaknesses

When I transitioned to my career in banking, I was able to use those strengths to build networks and open new geographical markets that the bank could invest in. Those strengths powered my new career. A skill that I completely lacked in the past turned out to be my main strength when I transitioned to banking. I didn't ignore a weakness—being shy—but faced it and worked through it. The secret formula was simple: I had followed my passion, and this time was using my experience in making a difference in the infrastructure market in developing countries. My passion was what helped me transform my biggest weakness (communication) into my biggest strength.

Like most people, I have strengths that I am not necessarily passionate about. For example, I've always been good with numbers. As a student I excelled at mathematics, algebra, and geometry. When I moved into banking, I was able to capitalize on that strength, including making complicated calculations in my head, while my colleagues relied on calculators to make the same calculations. They were impressed and I felt some satisfaction knowing I could deftly handle complex numbers. But it was never a passion.

I might have been good with numbers, but I certainly didn't want to spend my life working with them. My simple and clear answer was always a big "no." I get bored too quickly and lose patience when I have to work solely with numbers. *Spending my entire day on something I don't have a passion for, even if it is a strength, is not the right answer—for me or you.*

WHAT SHOULD YOU DO WHEN
YOU HAVE A NEW PASSION?

In my banking career, I had the opportunity to learn more about myself and explore other (new) passions. It was an opportunity for me to grow personally and professionally. Some of my senior colleagues advised me to stick with my strengths and focus on my communication and business development skills that I have extensive experience in. Instead, I focused on my weaknesses, turning them into strengths. At that time, I was passionate about venture capital, private equity, solar energy platforms, green finance, and more, which were weaknesses because I knew very little about them. And only by exploring them was it possible for me to turn some of them into my new strengths and rebuild my new life because of them. If I had listened to my colleagues, I would never have learned and grown as much as I have.

It is always a good idea to capitalize on your strengths and use them in your career, even if you aren't passionate about those strengths—you'll gain more confidence and earn a promotion or secure a new opportunity. I certainly did this when I transitioned from one career to another. I used my strengths from previous careers to give me a competitive edge as an outsider in a new career.

Having said that, to build your entire career on a strength that you aren't passionate about is a mistake and a recipe for failure. *Working on strengths that you aren't passionate about can cause burnout, boredom, stress, fatigue, and exhaustion.* Focusing only on your strengths and ignoring your weaknesses is settling for only what you know, while fearing the things you don't know. Focusing solely on your strengths means retaining the status quo, while potentially

Working on strengths that

you aren't passionate about can

cause burnout, boredom, stress,

fatigue, and exhaustion.

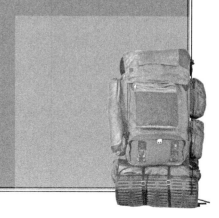

missing an opportunity to know how amazing you can be—if you would just give yourself a chance. It keeps you from entering the zone of genius we talked about earlier.

Focusing on only your strengths results in prioritizing short-term and short-sighted goals, while ignoring the long-term benefits that will eventually emanate from building your unique and special combination of strengths *and* weaknesses resulting from your passions. Focusing only on your strengths ignores the fact that change happens regardless of whether you maintain the status quo or explore new avenues. Working only on your strengths can instill a kind of lethargy in you.

On the other hand, your passions can help you turn weaknesses to strengths, often within a short time. Knowing and identifying your weaknesses is smart. And picking the ones that you need to work on to grow your passions more is even smarter. Prioritize long-term gains and master the art of learning new skills.

By turning your weaknesses into strengths, you open yourself to other opportunities when change happens. You will have more options and choices when you need to make a decision. Would you rather choose your destination, or be forced to stay where you are?

Turning your weaknesses into strengths gives you a power that other people might not have: the ability to integrate different kinds and levels of knowledge and becoming career shapeshifters™ or polymaths as we discussed in the first myth. *In the coming decades the world is going to need more knowledge integrators than ever.* Think about how many industries will probably become obsolete and extinct because of artificial intelligence or robotics. *Integrators of knowledge will be in a unique position to lead because they understand*

By turning your weaknesses into strengths, you open yourself to other opportunities when change happens. You will have more options and choices when you need to make a decision. Would you rather choose your destination, or be forced to stay where you are?

how to adapt to new situations and integrate knowledge coming from seemingly unrelated domains to come up with completely new and unique concepts. As Ernest Boyer, president of the Carnegie Foundation for the Advancement of Teaching, said, "The future belongs to integrators."

Turning your weaknesses into strengths makes you a better leader, one who can manage different types of teams. How can you manage a diverse team unless you have knowledge across different domains? It is also a call to have fun in life through new experiences and adventures. So far, I have been able to pursue several passions and enjoy several careers. I was able to build my strengths as an entrepreneur, a coach, a speaker, an app developer, an investment banker, a diplomat, a pharmacist, a singer, a soccer player, and probably in the future an astronaut—who knows what else.

Remember, this is not a call to do a bunch of things at the same time just so you can say you did them. Instead, it is just a call to follow your passions whether they show up in the form of a weakness or a strength. It is a call to enjoy what you are doing and become your most valuable asset.

MYTH BUSTERS

1. The muscle that you need the most is probably the one you haven't been working on, so, start training it now!

2. Focusing only on building your strengths can lead to mediocrity. You need to fix your weaknesses *before* you work on your strengths.

Myth #5 Focus On Your Strengths, Not Your Weaknesses

3. Work on your passions even if they lie in an area of weakness. Your weaknesses will eventually become your strengths, often in less time than you think.

4. Great leaders are brilliant at turning their weaknesses into strengths.

MYTH #6

Leaving Your Career is a "Sunk Cost"

"I want to look back on my career and be proud of the work,

and be proud that I tried everything."

— JON STEWART

The myth goes like this: Leaving your career is a sunk cost that you can't afford. When you move to a new career, you will lose everything you have built over years in your career, and you can't afford it, so it's better to stick to your current career.

Do you want to leave your career after all the years you spent in? Do you want to lose all that you have built over the years? Do you know how risky it is to leave your current career or build a business from scratch? Do you know that you will be forced to start at the bottom in your new career? Do you want to lose the status and power that you have in your current job?

These questions (and many more) will be part of the interrogation you will face from family and friends if you decide to leave your career and start fresh somewhere else. I heard these same questions over and over during my own career transitions. Most people think if they leave their careers to start a new one, they will have to start from ground zero, having wasted all of those years spent doing something else. In other words, they think whatever they had already invested in a career was a "sunk cost," and that they risk losing everything they have already invested. I thought the same thing when I moved from being a pharmacist to diplomat. What do you think?

Let me ask you something else: if you change careers, will your prior practical and personal experiences disappear? How about your personal skills? Will they all of a sudden become obsolete? I certainly thought that was the case. I thought everything I learned in school that wasn't directly related to diplomacy was wasted. Nothing could have been further from the truth.

MY OWN "SUNK COST" STORY

Over the course of my different careers, I have seen a lot of people who wanted change in their lives, but they felt stuck because they were afraid of losing the power and status they had already established in their current careers. During dozens of conversations I had with people and clients, I would hear pretty much the same answer: "Yes, I want to change. But I can't lose the power and the status that I have in my job and start over somewhere else. I will have wasted everything I have built over the years." Keep in mind that these were people whose ages ranged from thirty to fifty years old, so they included both experienced and less experienced professionals.

It took me ten years to discover it, but the truth is when you overestimate the benefits of the power and the status that you have in your current career, it can mask the potential as well as the benefits that you may gain from transitioning careers. *While you may think you are assuming less risk by maintaining the status quo, you may actually be inviting it: You risk overlooking skills that you can master in your new career, as well as future opportunities that may transform your life.* Most of us ignore our passions and stay where we are because we have become accustomed to what we have, or expect to get: the promotion or leadership position that is just around the corner. If we leave now, we'll be wasting everything we have invested so far.

In 2016, I was at the peak of my diplomacy career. At the time, I felt that everything was working the way I wanted it to. I was finally harvesting the fruits of my hard work after almost ten years. But I also found myself continuously asking, "What's next?" I was just about at the peak of my career, making it difficult for me to imagine what else I could do to stay at the top, and stay motivated. I tried to convince myself otherwise by telling myself I had a job with status and power, with more power waiting for me.

Here's the thing, though: when power controls your thoughts, you get disillusioned about what really matters to you. The mirage of more power and status distracts you from building the clarity needed for your vision. It distracts you from realizing which passions and values matter to you to live a purposeful life. That power makes your movements heavy because it is like adding weights to your legs. Even worse, you convince yourself that moving into a new career will be a sunk

While you may think you are

assuming less risk by maintaining

the status quo, you may actually

be inviting it: You risk overlooking

skills that you can master in your

new career, as well as future

opportunities that may transform

your life.

cost that you can't afford. And the more you spend in your current career, the more costs you add to that sunk cost.

Power is not always bad, except when it is the only thing that keeps you tethered to something you aren't passionate about. In that case, you are missing out. If you find yourself in this position, ask yourself questions like:

Do my passions lie in this new career?

Is it what I really want to do?

Does thinking about this make me feel happy?

Do I really see it feeding my life's purpose?

In my case, I decided that I needed a fresh start somewhere else, even if it meant losing the power I had spent years building. I needed to learn new skills and embark on a new challenge. To me, *challenges are the elixir of life: when you start a challenge and conquer it, you feel like you own the world.* I can't live without challenging myself and finding new dreams to achieve.

I knew I needed a new challenge, but I didn't know what I should (or could) do next. But life has taught me that when you are trying your best to reach inside your soul and find meaning in what you are doing, the universe will send you signals to follow to help you find that meaning or purpose. A few more months later I started receiving messages that helped me figure out what I should do next. First, it started with three people who didn't know each other, but they all delivered the same message to me, encouraging me to work for the Asian Infrastructure Investment Bank. When the first person told me this, I replied with an emphatic "no way"! When the second person told me the same thing a week later, I

Challenges are the

elixir of life: when you start a

challenge and conquer it, you feel

like you own the world.

thought, "Really. Does he mean it? He is the second person to say this to me." Two weeks later, another person encouraged me: "Why don't you consider working in that bank. I think you have the qualifications and the experience." This time, I responded: "Two other people told me the same thing recently." After several months I got the job. It was definitely a very challenging shift in my career life. But at the same time, it was one of the best decisions I have ever made. Yes, I did move down the hierarchy in my new career but the benefits I got and the skills I mastered during my four years there were more than worth it. My career in banking added another dimension to my personality and more importantly, I really enjoyed it.

I imagine what my life would be like if I closed my mind to the opportunities I had, or if I had ignored the messages I received. If I allowed fear to control me, I wouldn't have ever taken a chance. I would have told myself, "There's no way I can do this. I can't learn the skills needed to be a banker." Instead, I was open to new ideas and I didn't hold myself back from exploring. I told myself I didn't have anything to lose, so why not? I would never know what I was missing out on unless I took a chance.

The majority of us are afraid of big changes and tend to look the other way when facing them. *Changing your career may sound like a crazy, frightening thing to do. But you know what is really scary? Not reaching for your dreams and settling for a career that you don't enjoy. It is better to suffer temporarily in order to pursue your passions and dreams than it is to suffer long-term because you settled for a life or career that no longer fulfills you.*

Changing your career may sound like a crazy, frightening thing to do. But you know what is really scary? Not reaching for your dreams and settling for a career that you don't enjoy.

It is better to suffer temporarily in order to pursue your passions and dreams than it is to suffer long-term because you settled for a life or career that no longer fulfills you.

Myth #6 Leaving Your Career is a "Sunk Cost"

There is no such thing as a "sunk cost" when pursuing a new career or life. The time and effort you spend in a career is worth pursuing as long as you are enjoying it and are fulfilled. Once that stops and your passions change, it is time to move on. The real sunk cost is the time and effort that you spent doing something that you are no longer passionate about.

You probably think that a major part of any sunk cost would be the skills you built over the years that you would no longer use. In fact, I have learned that the skills you build over many years in one career are almost always transferable to your new career.

Let me give you a few examples of the skills I managed to keep using from one career to the other. One of the major skills I learned as a pharmacist was managing clients and building relationships with them. Despite the fact that I grew up shy and introverted, during my years in that industry, I learned how to build loyal customers who were willing to use our company's products and services. There were clients who bought from us only because of the personal relationship I built with them. This skill moved with me to my diplomacy career, enabling me to build strong relationships in a short period of time. I still use those skills today. You never know which connections will help lead you to your next destination.

I used the same skill when I moved into banking. Because of my strong communication skills built over my two prior careers, I was able to utilize this strength as a banker when building new client relationships. Capitalizing on my strengths was a tactic that I learned to use whenever I started a new position. As a bonus, I was put in charge of business development in the bank's investment department precisely because I brought a new perspective to my job.

I brought my experiences in handling relationships with government ministries and the private sector to the same table. I managed to build my networks very quickly in new markets and learned how to get the right investment opportunities; this led to opening new markets for the bank, especially in the Middle East. Yes, I had to learn other skills and get up to speed on the jargon of my new career, but my original skills were transferable from one career to the other. There were no sunk costs; instead, those skills were investments that paid off handsomely. I still use the same skills in my new career as an entrepreneur, business coach, and author and am so grateful to the experiences that I have been through in each and every career I have had—they all formed and shaped my unique experiences.

Here's another example. Do you see any connection between chemistry and Mandarin language? Probably not. Until recently, neither did I. I studied chemistry out of a passion for it, despite the fact that I also had a passion to become a diplomat. Organic chemistry taught me how to build a visualized memory, a process that involves remembering how to recognize and draw chemical compounds. It also taught me how to build a mind-map or visual-board for the entire organic chemistry sphere and do up to twenty-plus chemical conversions on my imaginary visual-board. Chemistry taught me that everything should have a logic, including how to draw each chemical compound. I learned how to draw each one using that logic, with drawing movements always starting from up to down and left to right.

What does this have to do with Mandarin? About eight years after studying chemistry, I moved to China to learn Mandarin. The

Chinese language was not like any of the languages I had learned before. Each language has a certain logic that makes it easy to learn once you understand that logic. I could learn Spanish and Italian by myself, because they have the same logic of French, which I learned in school. I learned Hebrew because it has the same logic as Arabic, my native tongue. But Mandarin was different, and I had to find logic to follow, so I could learn it quickly. The language doesn't have an alphabet and I had to memorize as many characters as I could, in order to start reading and writing. To my surprise, learning to read and write Chinese characters was easy for me. I was learning the language quickly compared to speaking it (speaking Mandarin was completely different from any language I had spoken before).

I didn't realize then why I was learning both reading and writing so quickly, but it gave me more time to focus on mastering the language. It was only years later when reading about "logical reasoning" that I was able to make the connection to chemistry. Confused? I'll explain, but first let me explain logical reasoning. Logical reasoning involves domains or careers that have some states of similarity, which help us make a connection between both domains: the new domain is more understandable by linking it to the one that is familiar to us. This concept has been widely used in research on science and learning new skills.

Writing Chinese characters is like drawing images and shapes. And drawing both Chinese characters and chemical compounds has more in common than I realized. In both cases, you start drawing from one direction to the other. Also, there is always a strong connection between the drawing and its meaning in Chinese, and the drawing and its chemical effect in chemistry. Moreover, the strong visualization memory that chemistry enabled me to build was instrumental in me being able to memorize Chinese characters in a very short time. I was able to use the same techniques and tactics that I used to use to memorize those chemical compounds.

When I left my pharmacy career, I thought that career was gone forever, including all the knowledge and the skills that I had. I was even questioning why I studied chemistry if my dream was to be a diplomat. I thought chemistry was a sunk cost for me that I would never recover. For a while, I thought that my peers in diplomacy were better than me because most of them were coming from a traditional diplomacy background. They studied these subjects in college, while I did something else. It took a few years for me to realize that this was actually the source of my strength, power, and uniqueness among my peers. I never imagined that learning chemistry would have made it easier for me to learn Chinese. Having a strong visual memory, I could use mind-mapping in my daily diplomacy work. I didn't know that I would be able to transfer my communication skills from my first career and build on and grow them through three other careers. Moreover, the medical knowledge and experience that I built in my pharmacy career saved my life more than once, and helped people around me in very difficult situations, including contracting COVID-19 and surviving it at home with self-medication.

When you are considering a career change, don't be afraid of the sunk cost that you would lose and miss forever. *Applying the law of conservation of energy (that is, energy is neither created nor destroyed) we can say, "your skills and experiences are not destroyed, nor do they vanish. They transfer and transmute with you wherever*

Applying the law of conservation of
energy (that is, energy is neither
created nor destroyed) we can say,
"your skills and experiences are not
destroyed, nor do they vanish.
They transfer and transmute with
you wherever you go." Every skill you
have built over the course of your
career can be transferred to
your new career.

you go." Every skill you have built over the course of your career can be transferred to your new career. Each experience you build in one career can be used and transferred to other careers. Don't lose sight of what your passions are and what really matters to you in your life, thinking that because of sunk costs you have to remain where you are.

Whether you realize it or not, you never start from zero when you start a new career. You start with your compiled and compounded experiences and skills that have been growing with you over the years. It is your past experiences and built-in skills which will make the difference in your new career or business.

MYTH BUSTERS

1. There is no such thing as a sunk cost when you consider changing your career or pursuing a new passion.

2. Skills and experiences don't vanish when you move to a new career. Instead, they transfer and transform to fit with your new career.

3. When you move to a new career, you don't have to start from zero again. You will start from where you stopped in your last stop. Move on!

MYTH #7

You Are Already in Your Dream Job

"Your career is like a garden. It can hold an assortment of life's energy that yields a bounty for you. You do not need to grow just one thing in your garden. You do not need to do just one thing in your career."

— JENNIFER RITCHIE PAYETTE

The myth goes like this: I am in my dream career. This is the best job in the world. I was never as happy as I am now—I'm going to do this forever.

Any dream job or career involves lots of components that need to come together:

1. You are doing something that you love and are passionate about.

2. You wake up every day excited to go to work; your work fulfills you.

3. Your job inspires you: you can see the impact you are having both within and outside your organization.

4. You have a great boss who trusts you implicitly and isn't afraid to delegate authority to you.

5. You have a great team that makes you feel like you are one of the family.

6. Your organization has a welcoming and inclusive corporate culture. You always feel valued.

7. Compensation packages are competitive.

8. Your job satisfies your core values and aligns with your personal values.

9. Your work and personal lives are balanced. You are able to enjoy pursuits outside of the office without feeling guilty or pressured.

These are the most important criteria you should consider when evaluating your job. On a scale from 1 to 10, if you score a 7 or higher for each criteria, congratulations—you are in your dream job. But what if you score below 7? What if you rank two or three criteria at a 10, but others a 1 or 2? Would your job still be considered a dream job? Let's say you were earning a competitive salary (maybe even one that is higher than you would expect in your field) but your colleagues are awful—would you still consider what you're doing a "dream"?

The truth is, even if you ranked all the criteria a 7 or higher, there's no guarantee that you will feel the same way in two, five, or even ten years from now. "Living the dream" depends on countless factors: your attitude, your boss, your teammates, your organization's culture, your HR manager, your organization's leadership team. You could be in your dream job for a few months before the company undergoes a major reorganization that changes your role completely, sometimes for the better but almost always for the worse. You may reach a career plateau where it's hard to see yourself progressing anymore, or you may simply become bored with what you're doing. You may even have no say in the matter— your company has decided to eliminate positions, including yours.

Sometimes things are within your control, but sometimes they are not. The COVID-19 pandemic that began in 2020 changed the entire global economy, and with it how people viewed work. Some people who were once satisfied with any job that would help them meet their financial obligations decided they wanted something more. The pandemic changed their perspectives toward working. As we discussed in the second myth, "Change Is Too Risky," change is a constant in life. Even if you are currently enjoying your dream job, be aware that that can change in a moment's notice.

I'm not being a pessimist, I'm being a realist. I wrote this book to inspire you to find work that is fulfilling at multiple levels—your dream career. But *understand that things don't always go according to plan: the world constantly changes, work environments change, people change, and we change, so why would we expect our dream jobs to remain static?*

As we discussed earlier, we need to embrace being career shapeshifters™ by being adaptable and agile when change hits. In a way, we need to predict change before it happens and pivot when we need to. We need to learn from previous experiences and not

Understand that things don't always go according to plan: the world constantly changes, work environments change, people change, and we change, so why would we expect our dream jobs to remain static?

be afraid to follow our passions. We need to be able to shift our career identity according to the circumstances we are facing. The result? More control over our lives and careers: we become the ones who decide when it's the right time to pivot and pursue that new opportunity.

Instead of focusing on the possibility that your dream job won't last forever, ask how you can continually adapt to the changes around you and be more in control—prepared to always be on the lookout for your next dream job. And, if you ever lose that dream job? Find your next one. *Life is a gift—don't waste it doing something you aren't passionate about.*

MY OWN "DREAM JOB" STORY

Applying the criteria listed above to my careers, I would say I have had a few dream careers. Pharmacy was never a dream career for me; I practiced it because that is what I studied. It gave me the ability to pursue my first dream career, as a diplomat. As I've said earlier, when I finally became a diplomat, it was one of the biggest and proudest moments in my life. It proved to me that I could realize my dreams and conquer the challenges I faced.

But like anything in life, careers have ups and downs. I've experienced both plateaus and peaks. After less than ten years in diplomacy, I felt that I had probably reached the pinnacle of my career. I had achieved a level of success that I never imagined. And I thought that if I couldn't do more than what I had already achieved, I would rather move on and learn something new.

As you can imagine, diplomacy is both interesting and challenging. It's still one of the most fascinating and diverse jobs I

Instead of focusing on the

possibility that your dream job won't

last forever, ask how

you can continually adapt to the

changes around you and be more

in control.

have ever had. My guess is that many people would consider being a diplomat a dream job. As you know by now, so did I. But every person has his or her own personal experiences. I thought I had gone as far as I could and was afraid if I continued on my current path, I would lose my motivation. I guess you could say my passion was waning.

I prayed for guidance on what to do next. Those prayers inspired me, and made me more aware and alert to new opportunities. I had learned early on that it is better to be prepared for an opportunity even if it never materializes than being presented with an opportunity for which you are unprepared.

As you know by now, my opportunity came from a start-up multinational development bank. It turned out to be my next dream job. I thought that working in the bank was a once-in-a-lifetime-opportunity—I either had to seize it or watch it vanish forever. To me, it was like working for the World Bank in 1944, when it was founded and just getting started.

If you are wondering how the heck a diplomat, with a degree in pharmaceutical sciences, would end up in the investment department of a multinational development bank, let me explain.

I have always tried to act on opportunities that come my way, even small ones. Three years before I was offered that dream job, and in addition to my current responsibilities, I was assigned to be the focal point of the Chinese outbound infrastructure projects in my country. The new task didn't involve any additional remuneration. It required working long hours every day on something I had no experience in. While others saw that new task as a burden and ran away from it, I saw it as an opportunity to learn something new and interesting.

The fruits of my labors were plentiful. In just three years, I built a wide knowledge base and expertise in infrastructure development, and developed a wide network of connections with banks, corporations, and government agencies. I grew my expertise by mixing and merging my diplomacy experiences with infrastructure development and investment, until the moment I was ready for my next big move.

This was one of the biggest lessons I learned in my life. If I hadn't taken on that smaller opportunity, I would never have been ready for the big one that knocked on my door three years later. I never looked at my responsibilities as a burden, because without them I wouldn't be learning and expanding my knowledge base, and I would not have been perceived as someone who could take on the next big opportunity. *Sometimes, the universe coordinates its actions in a magical and mysterious way. You won't get a big opportunity unless you get a smaller one first. If you don't act on that smaller opportunity, the bigger one will never materialize. But if you seize that small opportunity and give yourself a chance to move in a new direction, you will be able to see that big opportunity coming towards you and welcome it with open arms.*

When I started working in banking, it was definitely a dream job for me. I was enjoying what I was doing and having a positive and meaningful impact on developing economies, including my home country. I then decided to get my MBA with an intention to grow even more in my banking career. But to my surprise, studying for my MBA meant I was able to explore other new worlds and the careers available to me: marketing, operations, entrepreneurship,

Sometimes, the universe coordinates

its actions in a magical and mysterious

way. You won't get a big opportunity

unless you get a smaller one first. If you

don't act on that smaller opportunity,

the bigger one will never materialize. But

if you seize that small opportunity and

give yourself a chance to move in a new

direction, you will be able to see that big

opportunity coming towards you

and welcome it with open arms.

venture capital, and app development. Being exposed to these new worlds made me more intrigued to dive deeper into them.

Remember, your passions and interests shift all the time, and the dream job you have now may not be your dream job forever. And this is why I decided to pursue my entrepreneurship dreams, earning even more freedom in my life, and bringing my message to you. I felt that it was finally time to be my own boss. If I didn't try now, I would always wonder what I missed out on. I also felt that it would be selfish to keep my experiences to myself—my knowledge, wisdom, and experiences—instead of sharing them with others. It was a hard decision to leave both diplomacy and banking, but I knew I had to do it. The moment I stop chasing my dreams will be the moment I stop living.

MYTH BUSTERS

1. The only constant in life is change. Be prepared to pivot when your passions shift.

2. Your dream job might not last forever. If it doesn't, there's another dream job out there—if you look for it.

3. Use your experiences to be a career shapeshifter™. Remember, it's possible to enjoy more than one dream career in your lifetime.

Remember, your passions and

interests shift all the time, and the

dream job you have now may not be

your dream job forever.

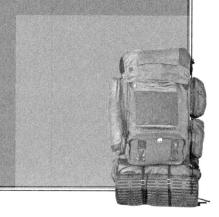

WHAT DID YOU THINK ABOUT
TIME TO MOVE ON?

I'd love to have your feedback about my book.

What did you enjoy? Is there something you wish

I had discussed more? Please feel free to send me an email at

dreamcareer@thepassionmba.com.

INDEX

ABOUT THE AUTHOR

Mustafa Ammar is the founder and CEO of The Passion MBA, a global coaching company. He is an entrepreneur and career and business coach who has helped hundreds of professionals around the world find their dream careers and build their dream businesses. Mustafa is a true career shapeshifter™. He started his career as a pharmacist as a result of his passion for chemistry. He then transitioned to diplomacy out of his passion for traveling the world and representing his culture and country, working in Malawi, China, and the United Nations. After reaching the peak of his diplomacy career, Mustafa transitioned to investment banking at the Asian Infrastructure Investment Bank, where he was in charge of business development and bringing investments to various regions around the globe, including Africa, the Middle East, and Latin America. His efforts contributed to attracting millions of dollars to the infrastructure market of these countries.

Based on his experiences pursuing his own different passions and successfully transitioning careers, Mustafa created *The Passion Blueprint*, a powerful and successful methodology that he has used to help clients support their own career transitions and find their next dream career or business.

FOR MORE INFORMATION

To learn how to devise that plan, join our ever growing community on Facebook group, The Passion MBA, Find Your Dream Career, or contact us at:

MustafaAmmar.com

ThePassionMBA.com

DreamCareer@ThePassionMBA.com

Follow us on Instagram @ThePassionMBA

Follow us on LinkedIn:
www.linkedin.com/in/mustafa-ammar-994a93120/

Join our Facebook community:
Find your dream career - The Passion MBA

The first step to know your dream career is to do "The Passionmeter" exercise. Download your free version from the exercise on https://thepassionmba.com/quiz-and-exercises.

Printed in Great Britain
by Amazon

32362286R00086